Race Contacts and Interracial Relations

Race Contacts
and Interracial Relations

LECTURES ON THE

THEORY AND PRACTICE OF RACE

Alain LeRoy Locke

Edited and with an Introduction by
Jeffrey C. Stewart

Foreword by Michael R. Winston

Preface by Thomas C. Battle

Howard University Press   Washington, D.C. 1992

MOORLAND-SPINGARN SERIES

Howard University Press, Washington, D.C. 20017

Copyright © 1992 by Moorland-Spingarn Research Center
and Howard University Press

Manufactured in the United States of America

This book is printed on acid-free paper.

10 9 8 7 6 5 4 3 2 1

Library of Congress Cataloging-in-Publication Data

Locke, Alain LeRoy, 1886–1954.
    Race contacts and interracial relations : lectures on the theory
and practice of race / Alain LeRoy Locke ; edited and with an
introduction by Jeffrey C. Stewart ; foreword by Michael R. Winston ;
preface by Thomas C. Battle.
    p.   cm.
    Includes bibliographical references.
    ISBN 0-88258-137-6 (cloth : acid-free paper) : $24.95. — ISBN
0-88258-158-9 (paper : acid-free paper) : $14.95
    1. Race relations.   2. Racism.   3. United States—Race relations.
4. Racism—United States.   I. Stewart, Jeffrey C., 1950–
II. Title.
HT1521.L595   1992
305.8—dc20   91-43415
                                                                  CIP

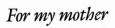

For my mother

Contents

Foreword

The publication of Alain Locke's *Race Contacts and Interracial Relations* provides scholars with an unusual opportunity. One of the enduring historical puzzles is how African Americans developed the intellectual resources to cope with one of the world's most sophisticated systems of racial domination. After the defeat of Reconstruction, public policy and private prejudice combined not only to deny the constitutional rights of African Americans, but also to destroy the educational and economic opportunities associated with genuine citizenship in a modern democracy. The imposition of white supremacy in every phase of American life was justified by wide dissemination of racist propaganda and supported by many of the leading white scholars and scientists of the late nineteenth and early twentieth centuries.

This tide of racial thought was opposed in many of its brutal anti-black aspects by African American intellectuals, but even so intrepid an opponent as W. E. B. Du Bois accepted some of its basic tenets about blood and racial genius in his 1897 lecture to the American Negro Academy on "The Conservation of Races." From the 1920s to the 1940s there was a "Copernican Revolution" in the way social scientists treated the concept of race. Many would attribute this change solely to the emergence of a new orientation in the social sciences opposed to Social Darwinism and biological determinism. More careful investigation, however, reveals that an important element of that change was the reshaping of the national debate about race and public policy by black scholars, the black press, and the National Association for the Advancement of Colored People.

What Locke's lectures on race contacts and interracial relations allow us to see is the embryonic formation of what would become a new consensus on race about thirty years later. Here is an early effort to analyze more than the argument and conclusions of racialist social thought. Alain Locke examines the assumptions or predicates of the theory itself, a quite different undertaking from the protests of the emerging civil rights intelligentsia. A striking effort on its own terms, it is all the more remarkable when one considers that Locke was not trained in the social sciences, was preoccupied with axiology and ethics in the field of philosophy, and was to spend much of his career as a leading critic of art, music, and literature. One recognizes in these lectures the extraordinary range of his reading and acquaintance with the relevant social science of his day. There is also in these lectures evidence of prescient intellectual groping. He expresses the hope, for example, that a genuine "science of human society" will emerge in the future and eliminate "false conceptions of race" that are an "obstacle to modern progress and a menace to modern civilization."

In tandem with Locke's dedication to a dispassionate examination of all the social phenomena associated with race is a very subtle understanding of the dynamics of a positive racial consciousness and achievement in a multiracial, multicultural society. In this respect also, he was far ahead of his contemporaries. An additional characteristic of Locke's discussion that should be highlighted is his consistent effort to place race in comparative perspective, citing European and Asian illustrations of some of his more suggestive points.

The Locke lectures on race contacts are also revelatory with respect to the evolution of his thought on historical and political matters. His conclusion, for example, that the Fourteenth and Fifteenth Amendments were "adopted before they were possible in point of fact" and "necessarily lapsed until the practical conditions could catch up with them" placed him in the ultraconservative camp of that era. Similarly, his assurance that he was "not an enemy of imperialism" informs us of how much his views would evolve in the subsequent decades of the 1920s and 1930s.

To make a proper estimate of the influence of Locke's evolving ideas on race and related issues it is useful to recall his role in the early 1930s as one of the founding fathers of the Division of the Social Sciences at

Howard University. Locke believed that philosophy as a discipline could play an extraordinarily constructive role in the twentieth century as an analytic adjunct of the social sciences. In addition to his placement of philosophy in the social science division at Howard, he was a prime catalyst in the division's conceptualization of problems for nearly twenty years. Locke's colleagues in the division included Ralph J. Bunche, E. Franklin Frazier, Abram L. Harris, and Rayford W. Logan, all leaders in their respective fields. All of them participated in the redefinition of race in the social sciences, shifting the emphasis from the older superficial biological claims to a more complex and empirical social concept of race.

Locke's lectures on race were an early indication of his conviction that "free, independent and unimposed thinking is the root source of all other emancipations." While Locke's own ideas about race shifted several times as the social sciences and humanities deepened our understanding of social heredity and culture, he was throughout his career committed to free inquiry and the forging of what he called "social intelligence."

Although these lectures were never prepared for publication by Locke himself, with all the enhancements and clarifications that he would have grafted on these preliminary and exploratory ideas about race, it is particularly fortunate that the lectures are now being published thanks to the extensive research and editorial work of Jeffrey C. Stewart, whose command of the resources documenting Locke's life and work is unparalleled.

Michael R. Winston

Preface

Race Contacts and Interracial Relations: Lectures on the Theory and Practice of Race, the five Alain Leroy Locke lectures edited by Jeffrey C. Stewart, is the culmination of a project conceived at the Howard University Moorland-Spingarn Research Center (MSRC) during the centennial year of Locke's birth. Locke (1885–1954), the first African American Rhodes Scholar, was first appointed to the Howard University faculty in 1912 and served until his retirement in 1953, with the exception of the period between June 1925 and June 1928. Although the Alain Locke Papers in the Manuscript Division of the MSRC have been the subject of much research in recent years, that research has focused primarily on Locke's involvement in the arts and humanities and their flowering during the so-called New Negro or Harlem Renaissance. Relatively little attention has been given to Locke's other intellectual and scholarly activities.

As a young faculty member at Howard University, Locke had been an early proponent of the university's greater involvement in academic programs exploring the history and cultures of African peoples in Africa and the African diaspora. He proposed the introduction into the curriculum of courses related to these subjects, but his efforts were unsuccessful. He did, however, present lectures that were designed to achieve a broader understanding of cultural diversity. It is the substance of these lectures that is presented here.

The transcripts that form the basis of Locke's lectures in this volume are a portion of the voluminous body of personal and professional papers that Locke bequeathed to Howard University upon his death in 1954. The Alain Locke Papers are an exceedingly rich resource for studying Locke's life and his various intellectual pursuits. Jeffrey C. Stewart, a scholar of the life and work of Locke and Locke's contemporaries, was selected to edit the essays because of his extensive knowledge of Locke and the Alain Locke Papers. In 1982, Stewart published *The Critical Temper of Alain Locke: A Selection of his Essays on Art and Culture*.

Race Contacts and Interracial Relations is one in a series of works undertaken under the auspices of the MSRC and published by the Howard University Press. The series presents works in a variety of formats and is designed to extend to a wider audience the rich resources of the MSRC and the fruits of its public programming. The MSRC is indebted to Jeffrey Stewart for this important contribution to the corpus of black intellectual thought.

Thomas C. Battle

Acknowledgments

My first acknowledgment must go to John Cell of Duke University. His comments on my paper and Alain Locke's pamphlet, *Syllabus to an Extension Course of Lectures on Race Contacts and Inter-Racial Relations*, at a 1978 American Historical Association meeting, led me to reconsider the importance of Locke's theory of race. That sparked curiosity about whether a comprehensive record of Locke's 1916 lectures on race existed, which bore fruit in 1982 when I discovered transcriptions of the lectures in the Alain Locke Papers of the Moorland-Spingarn Research Center at Howard University. Three years later, Thomas C. Battle, director of the Moorland-Spingarn Research Center, urged me to prepare the lectures for a Howard University publication to commemorate the hundredth year anniversary of Locke's birth. I am indebted to him and to such others as Clifford Muse, former acting director of Moorland-Spingarn Research Center; Caspa L. Harris, Jr., former vice president for Business and Fiscal Affairs; Michael R. Winston, former vice president for Academic Affairs; and William S. Mayo, assistant director of the Howard University Press for helping to get the project underway. I am indebted to Thomas C. Battle for his preface and for his support of the project in its final statges. I also wish to thank Michael Winston for his foreword and for many helpful suggestions concerning the final manuscript.

Because of a preoccupation with other commitments, I was unable to devote full-time attention to the project prior to the summer of 1988. In the intervening time, work began on editing the transcriptions, a process greatly assisted by Lawrence Lee Jones. His skill in deciphering words and in suggesting changes and additions was indispensable. Early drafts of my introduction also profited from his reading and suggestions. I also owe Kathi Ann Brown and Fran Wermuth, two students at George Mason University, a debt of gratitude for their assistance in research for the annotations during this phase.

More recently, I was assisted by professors Jack Censer, Marion Deskmukh, Hasia Diner, Prasenjit Duara, and Roy Rosenzweig of George Mason University who either commented on drafts of the lectures or suggested sources of information for the annotations. Special thanks are due Jane Turner Censer who made available to me her extensive knowledge and expertise as a historical editor and read drafts of the introduction. Jeffrey Butler of Wesleyan University was particularly generous in sharing his knowledge of English imperialism and South African race relations. Robert Hall of Northeastern University recommended readings in contemporary race theory, and Renate Reiss kindly agreed to produce a last-minute translation. I am particularly grateful to Walter A. Jackson of North Carolina State University who gave me many helpful comments on the entire manuscript. Members of the Working Group on African American History at Harvard University, especially Evelyn Brooks-Higginbotham of the University of Pennsylvania, provided insightful comments on the introduction. But extra special thanks go to Cheryl Simmons, a superb research assistant, who took the lead in conducting the extensive library research required for completion of the annotations. Special acknowledgment goes to Esme E. Bhan for her support and assistance during the research carried on in the Alain Locke Papers at Howard University. Two other librarians, Moore Crossey at Yale University Library and Kevin Proffitt at the American Jewish Archives in Cincinnati, dug up valuable information for the introduction and the annotations.

At Howard University Press the publication has enjoyed the sound advice, sure guidance, and unwavering support of Ruby M. Essien.

Final editing and revisions were made at the National Humanities Center, whose support, made possible by a grant from the National Endowment for the Humanities, allowed me to finish the manuscript. Steven Goldsmith and other members of the Working Group on Intellectuals and Politics at the Center made helpful comments on the Introduction, while Carmella Franklin gave me useful comments about textural editing. Thanks are due to Linda Morgan of the National

Humanities Center who typed a portion of the Introduction and to Rebecca Vargha and Jean Houston who tracked down books for me. I am particularly indebted to Jane Tompkins, who lent me her splendid printer during the last days of manuscript preparation.

My very special gratitude goes to Marta Reid Stewart, who has been my greatest source of strength, support, and encouragement in this and earlier labors.

Introduction

The Cultural Equivalent of Race

On the afternoon of 27 March 1916, a terrific rainstorm raged in Washington, D.C. and worried Alain Locke. Having entered the lecture hall in Carnegie Library on the Howard University campus, his wet umbrella in hand, he wondered who would attend the first of his five lectures on the subject of race that afternoon. Last year's audience for the lectures had been small and, even more disappointing, bereft of the more famous people at this well-known black university. He needed to reach a larger audience this time, especially one that included the influential people in the Howard University circle of deans. Locke had been the first African American Rhodes Scholar at Oxford and had joined the staff of the Teachers College at Howard University in 1912 as an assistant professor of the teaching of English and instructor in philosophy and education. He was now anxious to become a permanent member of Howard's more prestigious College of Arts and Sciences. But Locke also wanted to establish a course on race contacts and eventually an institute of race relations at Howard. As William Sinclair, a member of the Howard University Board of Trustees put it, Locke intended to pioneer at a black university the kind of sociology department that Columbia University was beginning to establish.[1]

Not everyone at Howard had supported Locke's plans. His five lectures on race contacts had first been proposed in 1914 but had not been given, because the board of deans had decided to limit them to only one evening.[2] After Jesse Moorland had donated his enormous collection of books and manuscripts of Afro-Americana to Howard University in December 1914, Locke had proposed that Howard inaugurate a research project to produce a bibliography of the collection and other works of "Negro Americana."[3] That request was not approved. Then in the summer of 1915, the board of trustees denied Locke's request to give his lectures as part of the regular curriculum.[4] Reportedly, the Board felt that Howard should avoid potentially controversial subjects such as race relations and confine itself to teaching the basic knowledge required to create teachers, doctors, and other professionals. But a younger generation of assertive black scholars was emerging at Howard, including Locke in English and later philosophy, Charles Wesley and Carter G. Woodson in history, Montgomery Gregory in drama, and Kelly Miller as dean of the College of Arts and Sciences, all of whom wanted Howard University to become a center for research and scholarship on African American life and culture. Undaunted by the initial opposition, Locke secured approval to present his material in the spring of 1915 outside the curriculum in a series of public lectures, under the auspices of the Howard Chapter of the National Association for the Advancement of Colored People (NAACP) and the Social Science Club.[5]

Delivered again in 1916, the series was a success. As Locke paced the stage for several minutes before beginning, the hall filled as people slowly came in from the heavy rain, hung up their raincoats, and settled into the hardwood seats of the lecture hall in Carnegie Library. The stenographer, a white George Washington University law student Locke had hired to record the lectures, sharpened his pencils and readied his pads while the compulsively punctual Locke looked nervously at his watch. By the time Locke delivered his opening remarks shortly after 4 p.m., the right people were there: Kelly Miller, the dean of the College of Arts and Sciences, and Lewis Moore, the dean of Locke's own Teachers College had arrived.[6]

Begun on the last Monday of March and continued each afternoon of the following four Mondays in April, Locke's lectures laid out his new sociological theory that race was not a biological but a historical phenomenon. Racial characteristics were not, as scientific racialists asserted, innate or permanent: "Anthropological factors are in themselves subject to change and perfectly unreliable as clues to any sociological meaning of the term 'race'[.]" Racial inequalities did exist but were unrelated to biological or anthropological factors, and instead "should be traced to historical causes and regarded as factors of a people's history." Even more dramatically, Locke argued that observers were wrong when they claimed that racism was inevitable and automatic: racism was a variable phenomenon, he observed, changing over time in response to economic, political, and demographic forces. Racism, or race practice as Locke called it, was not an instinctive response of American whites to blacks, but a "cultivated" phenomenon used by elites to foment tension and subjugate the less powerful. Locke not only cited American racial practices, but linked them to European imperialism, to anti-Semitism, and to discrimination against eastern Europeans in western Europe. After debunking common race creeds, Locke concluded his lectures by calling on "Afro-Americans" to develop their own race consciousness, like European ethnic minorities, as a powerful tool of advancement. Although race was an "ethnic fiction," it had survived, and would continue to survive, he told his listeners, because functionally, race consciousness gave groups a sense of "social solidarity" that aided their ethnic competition for power. He drew particular attention to artistic and cultural movements for self-determination in Ireland, Czechoslovakia, and Poland as models for the positive cultural consciousness he hoped African Americans would develop.

Locke's lectures were meditations on the worsening state of race relations in America. By 1916 the white South had segregated most public institutions, had denied blacks the legal right to vote, and had terrorized blacks with lynchings and race riots. When southern blacks migrated north during World War I to take jobs in St. Louis, Chicago, Pittsburgh, and Washington, D.C., they were met by more race riots both during and after the war. Even educated blacks such as Locke found the dining rooms of restaurants and dressing rooms of department stores closed to them in the nation's capital. And as if that were not enough, Woodrow Wilson, upon entering the White House, began to make segregation national by separating black and white workers in the federal government. In 1915 Wilson had D.W. Griffith's racist film of Reconstruction, *The Birth of a Nation*, shown in the White House. Later that year Colonel William Joseph Simmons of Atlanta, Georgia would revive the Ku Klux Klan after viewing the same film.[7]

Racist theorizing was on the rise by 1916 as well. Early twentieth century biological racists argued that immutable differences existed among the races, that blacks were biologically and permanently inferior to whites, and that Western civilization would decline if unrestricted intermixture occurred between blacks and whites. Some were Social Darwinists, such as Frederick Hoffman, a statistician working for the American Economic Association, who, in *Race Traits and Tendencies of the American Negro* (1896), used the flawed 1890 census to predict that blacks would soon die out in the Darwinian struggle of the survival of the fittest. Others were the intellectual heirs of Count de Gobineau, a nineteenth-century racist, whose theory that too much racial intermixture had brought about the decline of European civilizations was even more popular than Social Darwinism in 1916. His classic work, *Essai sur l'inégalité des races humaines* (1853–55) was abridged, translated, and published in the United States in 1915 as *The Inequality of the Human Races.* Four years earlier, the *Foundations of the Nineteenth Century*, a racist history written by Gobineau's disciple Houston Chamberlain, had also been translated and published in America. Paul Barringer, a University of Virginia professor, seemed inspired by Gobineau and Chamberlain when he wrote that blacks were in the process of genetic degeneration into criminal and immoral behavior following emancipation. These works rationalized the effort to segregate and disfranchise the black population, and they even suggested that the white population had a right to quarantine blacks to protect civilization.[8]

Nevertheless, contrary views on race, black character, and the societal consequences of racial interaction began to be heard in the first decades of the twentieth century, mainly from the pubescent disciplines of sociology and anthropology. The founders of the American school of sociology, such as Franklin Giddings, Charles Cooley, and Edward Ross, argued that the "inferior" traits of black people were caused by the environment and that blacks possessed the capacity to become more civilized. These sociologists were pessimistic, however, about changing the racist caste psychology of the white South. For these progressives, black character might be "reformed," but not white opposition to integration and to black advancement. William I. Thomas of the University of Chicago argued that the racial antipathy of the whites was tantamount to an inborn instinct, and was therefore fixed and unamenable to rational persuasion for progressive change.[9]

Opinion among black intellectuals was divided as well. After Booker T. Washington's death in 1915, most black intellectuals agreed with the demand for black political and social equality, but few agreed on the best means of achieving it. Some intellectuals, such as T. Thomas Fortune and John S. Durham, eschewed a racial analysis of the black situation in America and argued that African Americans represented a distinct social class. Although this class was unique because it had been enslaved, it was engaged in the same struggle as other white workers.[10] Like white progressives, these black intellectuals saw black advancement as a question of the freedman's ability to assimilate Anglo-American technical civilization as skilled individuals. Other intellectuals such as Alexander Crummell, John Bruce, and W. E. B. Du Bois believed that African Americans needed a positive conception of race to restore black self-esteem in the aftermath of slavery and Reconstruction.[11] Du Bois, a sociologist with a Ph.D. in history from Harvard University, questioned whether black culture should be sacrificed for the sake of social improvement. In "The Conservation of the Races" (1897), Du Bois argued that blacks shared political and economic values with other Americans but retained a unique spiritual temperament.[12] Race seemed permanent in Du Bois's view: "[I]n our calmer moments we must acknowledge that human beings are divided into races; that in this country the two most extreme types of the world's races have met."[13] Du Bois could not explain scientifically the existence of a distinctive beautiful black culture without positing a transhistorical concept of race: "[W]hile they perhaps transcend scientific definition, [races] nevertheless, are clearly defined to the eye of the Historian and Sociologist."[14] That position logically undercut the environmentalist argument that race differences were mutable and that blacks were thoroughly assimilable into Western society.

Most important to Locke's research, however, was the work of Franz Boas, the father of American anthropology, whose early studies of racial traits and whose pioneer volume, *The Mind of Primitive Man* (1911), revolutionized theories of race and culture. His paper "The Instability of Race Types," delivered in 1911 at the Universal Race Congress in London, established that physical characteristics of the races changed along with changes in the environment. Based on research he had undertaken for the U. S. Immigration Commission on the so-called new immigrants from southern and eastern Europe, Boas argued that physical traits of immigrants changed after years in the American environment and tended to approximate the American standard. Boas also asserted the mental and cultural plasticity of immigrants undergoing Americanization. Even more profoundly, Boas's pioneer work, *The*

Mind of Primitive Man, also published in 1911, deflated the Social Darwinist notion that non-Western societies represented primitive or earlier stages of evolutionary development. Dismissing the Social Darwinist belief in a hierarchical scale of culture on which various races could be ranked, Boas argued that each group possessed a culture, or set of beliefs, values, and practices, that was valid on its own terms. Civilization, according to Boas, was not advanced in isolation through independent inventions as the Social Darwinists claimed, but by the diffusion of ideas from one group or individual to another. Cultural interaction was the key to civilization building, and Boas's work moved anthropology away from studying the physical forms of various peoples to conducting fieldwork among non-Western cultures.[15]

In 1916, however, Boas's work was known only to a handful of Americans: the diffusion of Boas's ideas would come through his professorship at Columbia University, where he would train a generation of graduate students, such as Melville Herskovits, Ruth Benedict, and Margaret Mead, who would popularize his work in the 1930s and 1940s. But in the 1910s Locke was the intellectual who most fully comprehended the implications of Boas's theories for African Americans. Locke realized that this material revolutionized racial science by shifting the burden of proof onto the racists and taking from them the sanction of anthropology. Moreover, in these lectures, Locke presented what historian Thomas Gossett has stated was most needed by the "defenders of the Negro" during the World War I era—"a direct challenge to the intellectual bankruptcy of racist theory. Without such a challenge, one which would make sense to the hard-boiled disciplines of biology, anthropology, sociology, and psychology, the battle to improve the status of the Negro was a thankless and almost hopeless task."[16]

This challenge Locke supplied. In lecture 1, "The Theoretical and Scientific Conceptions of Race," Locke utilized Boas's work to argue that anthropology had been unable to isolate any static factors of race. Race was not a fixed, biological entity because the physical characteristics of racial groups changed with alterations in social and cultural environment and even varied considerably within groups. Going even further than Boas had in 1911, Locke asserted that biology had no influence on race types. Race was simply another word for a social or national group that shared a common history or culture and occupied a geographical region. Race was culture, because "every civilization produces its [own] type." This formulation actually anticipated Ruth Benedict's *Patterns of Culture* (1934), in which she described races as so much putty in the hands of culture.[17] In a sense, then, Locke was standing racialist theories of culture on their heads: rather than particular races creating Culture, it was culture—social, political, and economic processes—that produced racial character.

Locke can be credited, therefore, with removing race from its biological basis and putting it squarely on a cultural foundation. Boas continued to believe that hereditary factors played a role in race, whereas Locke had extended Boas's observations of racial variability into a thoroughgoing environmentalist view that there were "no static factors of race."[18] Locke saw that races, as products of culture, were constantly undergoing change. Rather than viewing blacks and whites as extremely different types as Du Bois had done, Locke saw blacks and whites as highly assimilative beings: blacks had assimilated Anglo-American culture to a large degree, just as whites had imbibed African American culture. Pre-Boasian theories of culture claimed that an inherited racial genius created Western civilization, a position that Du Bois inadvertently reinforced when he argued that black culture was a product of a black "genius." The ongoing process of cultural exchange and interaction under slavery had made white and black Americans basically similar from a cultural standpoint. Whatever was distinctive about black culture was a product of the particular historical and cultural conditions of black life in America and the cultural characteristics Africans had brought with them on the slave ships.

Yet Locke's theory diverged sharply from Boas's in two ways. First, Locke differed from Boas on the question of the value of race consciousness. Boas believed that the solution to the racial problem required that we deemphasize race in modern life and assimilate ethnic groups totally into the dominant American stock.[19] But Locke wished to retain the concept of race. He did not accept the proposition that race was either a permanent biological entity or nothing at all: people often possessed a race or group sense that contributed to group esteem and power. Second, Locke moved beyond the cultural relativism of Boas to analyze race within the context of modern imperialism. For Locke, race was not simply a theoretical question, but a practical issue affecting social relations in the United States. Although American anthropology under Boas criticized intellectual racism in the early twentieth century, it never produced a comprehensive critique of Western imperialism, which was

rapidly absorbing non-Western peoples into what Immanuel Wallerstein called the "world system."[20] Locke recognized that for peoples of
color in the twentieth century the issue of race was linked to the reality
of modern imperialism and saw how that imperialism affected their lives
and cultures.

Locke's *Race Contacts* is exciting because it addressed that issue in
lecture 2, "The Political and Practical Conception of Race." Locke
placed the discussion of race within the context of European imperialism: race defined one's relationship to power under modern
imperialism. Ideas of race might be mythic constructions of reality, but
they were rooted in a race *practice* of discriminatory treatment that had
existed since ancient times. As Locke put it, "The practices of race are
world old, and only the theory is modern." Imperialism was the practice of race, the domination of one group by another group, which
invoked the ancient kinship sense of "blood is thicker than water" or of
"us" versus "them" to give European nations a sense of solidarity (the
"French race" was a popular construction of the time). Such conflicts
in the ancient world had been merely ethnic competition for scarce
resources; however, in the modern world they were fueled mainly by
economic competition between nation states that used race consciousness to justify exploitation of others. Modern imperialism, then, was a
new system of exploitation, one that organized power on the basis of
color: only since the fifteenth- and sixteenth-century expansion of Europe through the slave trade had color become the prime indicator of
racial status in the modern world. In addition, modern imperialism
relied on racial theories to justify its practices: non-Western peoples
were defined as culturally inferior and thus deserving of conquest and
exploitation. Under such circumstances, even missionaries became in-
sidious tools of imperialism, as they consciously or unconsciously deval-
ued indigenous cultures and created markets for Western goods by
bringing a "superior" Christian religion and culture to the "natives."
Notions of racial inferiority, therefore, directly fueled the economic
development of the West and the underdevelopment of non-Western
peoples.

Locke approached race as Karl Marx had analyzed class—as the vortex
of modern social relations. For Marx, classes resulted from the mode of
production in a society, and thus were dynamic, changing with changes
in the organization of production, such that a people were divided into
lord and serf, landlord and tenant, or capitalist and worker depending

on the mode of production that dominated the economy of a society. For Locke modern races resulted from the *praxis* of modern imperialism, which defined as "inferior" those races such as Arabs, Africans, East Indians, and African Americans who were unable to free themselves from colonial subordination. Even those peoples such as African Americans who were not directly subject to an empire were subjected to the imperial attitude on the part of Anglo-Americans. Imperialists exploited race differences to sustain political, social or economic disparities between European and non-European colonials. Such disparities were real, as an honest analysis of the conditions of life under colonialism revealed. As Marx himself observed of American slavery, "the overworking of the negro and sometimes the using up of his life in 7 years of labour became a factor in a calculated and calculating system . . . [for the] production of surplus-labour."[21] By the early twentieth century imperialists were able to capitalize on race differences to overwork Asians, Africans, and other non-Europeans and wring more surplus labor from them than from European laborers. Such an economic advantage fueled the "race practice" of imperialism. Although Locke did not attempt the rigorous investigation of the economic origins of imperialism that V. I. Lenin provided in *Imperialism: The Last Stage of Capitalism* (1917), Locke's analysis did anticipate Lenin's acknowledgment in the "Preliminary Draft Theses on the National and Colonial Questions" (1920). There Lenin backed the notion that oppressed colonial and national minorities such as blacks in America had a right to self-determination. Locke's lectures provided one of our earliest analyses of colonialism from the standpoint of the colonized.[22]

Locke extended his critique to the subject of race conflict *within* a society in lecture 3, "The Phenomena and Laws of Race Contacts." Here he looked at the surface issue of color and asked what it represented. What historical forces had made color relationships the way they were? The answer lay beneath the appearance of race conflict, because "all such problems and issues originate, after all, not in the mind, but in the practical problems of human living." In many cases racial categories were simply class categories that had become hereditary. Economic competition between ethnic groups was often the underlying cause of racial conflict and perhaps the key to understanding why racial conflict increased or subsided in relation to poor or good economic conditions. Indeed, one of the reasons for the ebb and flow of racial feelings and conflicts was that elites manipulated race feelings to divide and control the working classes. Locke's perception of how economic conflict shaped race relations led to his most important observation about race contacts within a society: race feelings changed over time in response to changes in historical conditions. Racism actually changed, or passed through distinct phases, often in response to varying economic conditions in a society.

Yet in lecture 3 Locke also moved beyond the notion that race was solely a function of economics: racial feelings also changed with the removal of formal social barriers to contact or with dramatic changes in population. Often such alterations triggered a racial response from those peoples who believed themselves to be in control. The relation of race to population suggested that something more than simply class, and perhaps even more than naked political power, was at stake in the reactions of race. Racism was not only a reflection of class interests but also a cultural system that reflected the social psychology of a people. Race feelings often intensified with perceived changes in social status. Ironically, even attempts to reform race relations, such as the passage of laws or amendments to the Constitution, failed to eliminate race problems and instead elicited new racial responses that propelled relations into another phase. Legal recognition of race distinctions sometimes fixed in time an attitude or practice that might otherwise have passed off the map of racial practice. Most important, the dominant group in a society, despite its political and economic power, could not completely control race contacts: the submerged groups could assimilate into or distinctively color the culture of the society despite such restrictive measures as segregation. In an analysis that was again indebted to Boas, Locke observed that cultural exchange between the dominant and subordinate races could not be arrested, with the result that the national identity or "civilization type" produced was inevitably a joint product.

Race contacts were not, therefore, simply a mystification of class antagonism, as many twentieth-century Marxists claimed, but a complex set of responses by groups to beliefs, values, and cultural perceptions that sometimes did not follow economic interest. Sometimes a region such as the South, or a class such as white workers, acted against its own economic interests in a seemingly blind attempt to maintain a benighted racial superiority. The question was not whether racism was a trick played by capitalists on the working classes, but why race was such an effective divisive tactic. Sometimes racial violence or discrimination was a response to the greater intimacy between groups brought on by economic consolidation. Locke invoked a rudimentary version of the "psychological strain" theory—that ideologies take hold in communities or individuals that feel threatened—to account for the attractiveness of racist attitudes.[23] Such stress had existed since the European expansion of the fifteenth and sixteenth centuries, which had disrupted traditional hierarchies as the social standing of elites became more tenuous. As had de Tocqueville before him, Locke argued that race prejudice was particularly prevalent in democratic societies, where, in the absence of aristocratic—and hence, hereditary—barriers, society created analogous ones in race discrimination. Race revived dormant but deep associations with tribe and nation, especially during periods of group stress. Such feelings spread and infected the entire group when it felt its collective survival threatened. Race, therefore, was really a tribal or national sense that had nothing to do with color.

To support this view, Locke compared American racism with European ethnic conflict in lecture 4, "Modern Race Creeds and Their Fallacies." Racism was a special version of ethnic tension, different in degree but not in kind from the ethnic conflicts that erupted among Europeans. Locke cited European anti-Semitism, French-German tensions in the Rhineland and in the Alsace-Lorraine district, and Austrian discrimination against the Slavic peoples as evidence of intra-European prejudice. In one case Locke related how a Lithuanian could "pass" and obtain service in Austrian restaurants if he could disguise his accent. If the accent revealed the Lithuanian's ethnicity, however, then he would encounter discrimination, "showing after all [that] any arbitrary, artificial factor can control the situation [even though] color by its very obviousness makes the [reaction] more virulent than perhaps any other single factor. Those, therefore, who are subject to a color discrimination are simply the easy victims of a force in human society which operates along lines of other factors wherever there is this conscious indoctrination of race."

Turning to Europe also provided Locke with comparative confirmation of his observation that ethnic tensions lay dormant until they were cultivated, even indoctrinated, in the population by "a certain class . . . interested in its deliberate maintenance [, interested] that the system of racial hatred should not die out even after the growth of it has died down." This situation was definitely the case in the Rhineland and in the Alsace-Lorraine district, which witnessed "a deliberate outcropping of that same kind of [group antipathy caused by external] influence that [in its] most virulent form cannot be more virulent than the question of racial [conflict,] proving it seems, our view [that] indoctrination can operate to such an extent that over certain issues racial antipathies can actually spring up between divergent sects or divisions of the same race or the same ethnic strain."

Locke's parallelism between ethnic and racial conflict received unexpected confirmation in 1916. Just six months after Locke delivered his lectures, Madison Grant published *The Passing of the Great Race*, which argued that the different European regions were populated by different races.[24] Europeans were not of one race, but consisted of the Alpines of eastern Europe, the Mediterraneans of southern Europe, and the precious Nordics of northern Europe and Scandinavia. Advocating that America adopt a strict immigration policy, Grant repeated Gobineau's warning that societies declined when they allowed too much intermixture with inferior race groups. Following the logic of Locke's theory, Grant's book signaled that as competitive industrial capitalism had drawn larger numbers of immigrants to the nation, an intensification of racial feelings and now formalized creeds of ethnic difference had emerged to justify discriminatory practices. Grant's book also signified the changing climate of scientific opinion: Grant made few references to physical characteristics, perhaps in recognition of the decreasing foundation for such analyses in contemporary anthropological circles.

In lecture 4 Locke abandoned the purely descriptive posture of the social scientist and began to critique racial creeds. Just as Marx had observed that the dominant class seeks to stabilize its position by creating an ideology that rationalizes its position, so too Locke knew that racial creeds not only justified dominance but encouraged subordinate groups to accept such dominance. Exposing the faulty reasoning of the predominant race creeds of his day had the long-range effect of demystifying the claims of intellectual racists. But Locke also believed that race creeds would persist in society as long as the practice of racism was successful and profitable in competitive industrial societies. Although like some early twentieth-century Marxists, Locke believed that the competitive industrial system would ultimately make racial segregation economically anachronistic, he also knew that the virus of racism had spread so completely in the United States that it would continue to exist despite countervailing economic pressures. Racial attitudes would remain for a long time, even though they might eventually die out once society transcended the exploitive competitiveness that characterized the period of European expansion and imperialism. Were not blacks condemned to lose in competition with other groups for the rewards of American life, because they lacked the political and economic power to alter prevailing American practice? Certainly Locke was no revolutionary, and he did not advocate the overthrow of the American social order. He noted that society typically sought a *modus vivendi* between contending groups: the currently accepted American solution was segregation, which even some blacks, such as Booker T. Washington, tried to turn to their advantage. Political and legal equality would be realized, Locke believed, but only after historical conditions had become more favorable to blacks than they were in 1916. What could blacks do besides wait for change or attack the American social order?

Locke's answer to that question appears in his last lecture 5, "Racial Progress and Race Adjustment," and followed two lines of analysis. The first suggested that the resolution of racial divisions came when a society develops a "civilization type" that melds the various social races or social groups. Because "every civilization tends to mould its own type," there was evidently an American type: Boas had argued that the physical characteristics of immigrants changed in the American environment and moved closer to those of the typical American. Locke argued that Jews and blacks were successfully assimilating the dominant culture's mores, values, and behaviors, and he recommended that African Americans continue to assimilate in order to progress. Cultural conformity was a must for the survival of any minority, Locke argued, and he seemed to nod to Booker T. Washington in using the word "adjustment" to characterize race progress as dependent on the African American's willingness to adopt American middle-class values. Locke's notion of a "civilization type" also embodied the Enlightenment's ideal of progress toward a cosmopolitan "civilization" that transcended national and racial boundaries. In such a world, willingness to assimilate, in terms of the exchange of cultural values, would become the key to "culture-citizenship."

But Locke rejected total assimilation as a solution to America's racial problems. Comparing Japanese and African American attitudes toward Western assimilation, Locke commended the Japanese for taking the technical insights of the West without repudiating their own traditions. Locke was a pluralist, who believed in the right of a culture to pursue its own development, to be taken on its own terms, and to resist being crushed into unity and conformity. Like Johann Herder, Locke saw the value of belonging to a group and preserving one's own culture.[25] The values of the minority group were neither strictly commensurate with nor always inferior to those of the dominant group in a society, and they should not be trampled in the rush to assimilate. In a passage that showed some indebtedness to W. E. B. Du Bois, Locke called for a conservation of the best attributes of the race, by instilling in the "representative classes" a sense of race solidarity and loyalty. Racial pride for the group, Locke suggested, was the social analogy of self-respect for the individual: it was a powerful ideological tool for building group esteem and solidarity in competitive societies. That race was a biological fiction should not prevent African Americans from appropriating its more legitimate, social meaning—as social race, as a metaphor for group or national identity—to empower their own development. Locke argued that this stimulation of race pride was not paradoxical, but actually the key to stimulating the self-respect of the group to strive to meet the common standard of the society as a whole. For in an analysis that paralleled Marx's distinction between a class in-itself and for-itself, Locke argued that African Americans could not simply remain a race held together by common condition; they must become self-consciously a race for-itself, bound together by a common consciousness of its real position as a group in modern social relations.

What distinguished Locke's recommendation of race consciousness in 1916 was his emphasis on the arts and letters as the vehicle for African American racial progress. Drawing again from European examples, Locke argued that "[t]he Celtic [and] the Pan-Slavic movement[s] in arts and letters—movements by which the submerged classes are coming to their expression in art—seem to be the forerunners of that kind of recognition which they are ultimately striving for, namely, recognition [of an] economic, [a] civic, and [a] social sort; and these [movements] are the gateways through which culture-citizenship can be finally reached." Like European minorities, African Americans could compensate for their thwarted political aspirations for self-determination by empowering themselves through a cultural ideology. Through art blacks could build social solidarity and race consciousness, without overtly threatening the white power structure. Moreover, by developing their cultural productivity, blacks would contradict the notion that African Americans were a people without culture, whose only choice was complete assimilation. Here, then, was Locke's theory of the social use of art to attain culture-citizenship, which would become the basis for his advocacy of the New Negro Renaissance of the 1920s.

Locke's recommendations showed his pragmatism, just as his rejection of assimilation showed his pluralism. As did William James, Locke saw the world as an open pluriverse in which humanity had the ability to shape its world. Thus, while he drew the outlines of a science of racial interaction, he rejected, again as did James, any determinism, especially a racial determinism which, on the one hand, bound blacks to biology, and on the other, stultified black activism because of the socially unyielding power of racism. Despite his appreciation of Marxism and his recognition that racist ideas and attitudes followed social practice, Locke was unwilling to rule out the possibility that even blacks, though seemingly powerless, could not alter the social situation through their own actions. Indeed, his analysis had shown that assimilation and exchange between blacks and whites had continued, even flourished, under segregation despite attempts to control contacts between the races. Culture did not always follow power, but often was an indirect way for the racial minority to subvert and sometimes to control the racial majority. The American slave, for example, had shaped the master's language, folkways, and general culture in the antebellum South and had contributed significantly to the American "civilization type," even though it was generally unrecognized and unacknowledged in Locke's day.[26] But by arguing for the creation and recognition of a distinctive African American culture, even when Locke's own analysis reflected the overwhelming assimilationist stance of most black people, Locke was acting like a good pragmatist and inventing a racial tradition whether or not one existed. For pragmatically, blacks needed a culture to enhance their status and bolster their competition with other groups through art.[27]

Locke's pragmatic approach to the problem of race reminds us of James's approach to the problem of war in "The Moral Equivalent of War": Locke offered a cultural equivalent of race to his audience, both as a way for blacks to empower themselves and as a substitute for the more pernicious forms of race feeling and practice.[28] Just as James sought to create a substitute for the martial spirit that he felt would also remain in humanity, so too Locke envisioned a racially enriched art and culture as a healthy substitute for the vicious aspects of a racial instinct he believed would be around for a long time.

Unfortunately, Locke's innovative approach to race had little immediate impact in 1916. When he concluded his final lecture, there was little response from the Howard community, which was actually more concerned with other issues. During the second week of Locke's lectures, a student strike had erupted on campus and had consumed the attention of the faculty, the deans, and the board of trustees for nearly two weeks. This strike was a dress rehearsal for the more serious protest of 1925, when students again rebelled against what they believed was arbitrary discipline at Howard. With Booker T. Washington dead, the New Negro was in a protest mood, and Du Bois and the NAACP dominated African American thought. Locke's posture of scientific objectivity, on the one hand, and cultural expressiveness, on the other, was not the political fashion. As his friend Montgomery Gregory teasingly wrote to him after his lectures, "We wished for the sociological expert with his personal disinterestedness and notebook!!!"[29]

Of all those who attended, Kelly Miller may have been the person who most appreciated Locke's contribution, although even he had been only sporadically in attendance. Miller had written a scathing critique of President Wilson's policy of segregation and had lectured before the Washington, D.C., Mu-So-Lit Club in 1915 on the impact of World War I on race relations.[30] Miller sympathized with Locke's advocacy of increased race consciousness and respected the scholarship Locke had reviewed in compiling the lectures. Miller had approached Locke about lecturing in a course on sociology Miller planned for the fall, which would include lectures by Robert Park, the Chicago sociologist, whose work Locke had reviewed in his lectures.[31]

But Locke declined the invitation. Now that the lectures were over and his pamphlet, *Syllabus to an Extension Course of Lectures on Race Contacts and Inter-Racial Relations*, had been published, Locke was moving on: that fall he would be in residence at Harvard University, where he would earn his Ph.D. in philosophy within two years. Advancement for him lay in the direction of increased academic prestige, not continued lecturing on the widening influence of imperialism and capitalism on race practice. In the postwar years, he would be known as the dean of the New Negro Renaissance, but not for his pioneering sociological theory of race. Although an abbreviated form of the lectures would be given at Fisk University in 1928 and ideas from the lectures would inform his anthropology and sociology articles published in obscure journals, the lectures would remain unpublished and unnoticed for the rest of Locke's professional life.

Alain Locke
1885–1954

St. Clair Drake has said that a man proposes the kind of revolution his temperament permits.[32] Yet the cultural revolution Locke proposed seems paradoxical given his sociological analysis of race. After showing that race was a myth, both as a physical homogeneity and as a predictor of social behavior, Locke appears to resurrect race as a source of liberation from oppression in America. Perhaps even more paradoxical is his choice of art as the avenue for this racial salvation. After documenting that racial attitudes are largely reflective of racial practice, which is driven by economic and political forces, how could Locke believe that art and literature could alter black existence in a racist society? Even more mysterious, Locke never published his bold sociological lectures. Why did Locke not develop them further into a full-length book later in his career?

Perhaps Locke's biography will help resolve some of these paradoxes, for the five lectures of *Race Contacts* may have been an attempted resolution of a series of personal yet ideological conflicts that had roots in what Erik Erikson calls the psychosocial predicament.[33] Locke delivered these lectures when he was thirty years old, at a time when he was fashioning a mature social role for himself as well as defining his intellectual identity in America. Locke appears to have been struggling not only with the problem of race in modern society but also with the problem of social role for a black intellectual. How was a Harvard- and Oxford-educated black intellectual to improve the black situation, to realize his own potential for individual success, and to prosper in American society?

Locke had been a brilliant student in elementary and secondary schools, inspired partly by the model of achievement of black Philadelphians. That city had produced Henry O. Tanner, internationally renowned artist; Richard T. Greener, the first black graduate of Harvard College; and Dr. Caroline Still Anderson, the first woman physician of Philadelphia. Locke's parents were school teachers, increasing the weight of tradition behind his decision to become an educator; also, a professional career was this class's chief defense against prejudice: to succeed proved oneself the equal of whites and brought esteem to the race. Race representativeness meant that blacks should always put their best foot forward and present a genteel view of black life to the world.

Cultured individuals contradicted prevailing white opinion that all blacks were uneducated and ill-mannered. By attending Harvard, Oxford, and the University of Berlin, Locke distinguished himself and his race and fulfilled the goals of the black middle class.[34]

Indeed, when Locke arrived at Harvard College in 1904, he epitomized his suggestion in *Race Contacts* that successful minorities must assimilate the civilization in which they live. Majoring in English literature and philosophy, Locke was an Anglophile whose dress, manners, and demeanor made him a Black Victorian.[35] Intellectually, Locke still believed in an Arnoldian hierarchy of culture, that those who could appreciate the best that had been thought and created were superior to those who could not. Yet the paradoxes of being African American in the midst of Anglo-American culture were beginning to present themselves. He took courses from such professors of English as Barrett Wendell, who, though a Francophile, argued that modern literature had been a series of national literatures based on national traditions since the Renaissance, and that despite its current inferiority, American culture needed its own indigenous tradition. That concept inspired Locke to begin to imagine what a black literary tradition would look like and to think through how African Americans could make a distinctive literary contribution to American culture. Locke understood early in his career that if he wanted to become a black critic, he needed a black tradition to stand behind him. In the socially integrated world of Harvard, Locke began to develop a theory of the importance of loyalty to one's racial tradition for African American writers. Wendell, with his notions that the nineteenth century was a period of nationality in literature, encouraged Locke to think creatively about how he could create conditions for the emergence of an African American tradition in literature.[36]

Locke's study of philosophy as a Harvard undergraduate strengthened his sense of purpose without removing the creative tension between assimilationism and nationalism in his thought. From George Herbert Palmer, Locke imbibed the notion that the self cannot realize itself in isolation, but must devote itself to a higher, universal cause in order to achieve a larger selfhood. Locke's philosophical mentor, Josiah Royce, inspired him to give primacy to transcendental unity over empirical multiplicity in his view of philosophy and social reality, and to consider differences, even racial ones, as primarily matters of degree rather than of kind. And Horace Meyer Kallen, a Jewish graduate assistant in a course in Greek philosophy that Locke took as a senior, exposed him to the pragmatic pluralism of William James, as Locke did not take a course from James as a Harvard undergraduate. Kallen, who saw himself as the heir to William James, recalled having a series of conversations with Locke about the significance of racial differences, dialogues that began at Harvard and continued into the following year when both were at Oxford University. The phrase "cultural pluralism," or the right of ethnic groups to maintain their cultural distinctiveness, apparently emerged out of their conversations during 1907–08.[37]

But Locke does not appear to have fully embraced cultural pluralism at Harvard College. Kallen recalled that Locke would not give up the idea that different ethnic groups would ultimately assimilate into a universal "Man" (or what Locke himself would later call the "civilization type" of a society in *Race Contacts*). Although Locke never completely abandoned the hope that a "New Man," as de Crevecoeur had put it,[38] might emerge out of the interaction of races in America, he did become more sympathetic to the notion of cultural pluralism, especially after he went to Oxford as the first African American Rhodes Scholar in 1907. At Oxford, Locke confronted blatant and unyielding racism for the first time in his life. Rhodes Scholars from the southern United States succeeded in having him barred from the traditional Thanksgiving Dinner celebration held by the American Club at Oxford. Locke developed a deep resentment for these southerners and for some of the British, who were also very color conscious. Even though he enjoyed more cordial relations with his English undergraduates, most of the English elite not only snubbed him but also other colonial students. Here was the "Imperial Training School" Locke referred to in lecture 2 of *Race Contacts*. And here was the reality of difference, not as an abstract philosophical principle, but as a relentlessly enforced practice of dominance and subservience that made his Oxford years painful ones.[39]

Such experiences undermined the credibility of the black bourgeoisie's faith in assimilation as the key to success. The English, in his eyes, were no more cosmopolitan than the ignorant American southerners: both used power to block access to material and spiritual resources and justified such action by claims of inherent superiority. Contact with colonial students at Oxford, such as H. E. Alaily, president of the Egyptian Society of England; Pa Ka Isaka Seme, a black South African student of law; and Har Dayal, an idealistic revolutionary from India, helped Locke to place his experience and the black problem in a larger context. Not only were they responsible for his knowledge of imperialism and colonialism, but they may have introduced him to socialism and anticolonialist critiques of imperialism. Har Dayal, whom Locke met in connection with the Oxford Cosmopolitan Club, became a Marxist revolutionary in exile from India. Others, such as his close friend Seme, were intellectual nationalists, who saw themselves as developing culture and nationalism among their people when they returned home from Oxford. These intellectuals were painfully aware of the disparity between European and colonial social development, yet sensitive to the destruction of their native cultures under colonialism. As men of culture, their decisions to affirm their cultures was an effort to save their personal psyches as well as articulate the conditions for a national rebirth of their people. Embracing race consciousness and placing his own experience within the context of world wide imperialism, Locke began to conceive of a future role for himself as a leader of his own people.[40]

Fed up with Oxford and the English, but unwilling to return to the United States, he left England in 1910 and settled in Berlin, where he attended the University of Berlin, and traveled throughout eastern Europe. At the university, he continued the study of Kantian philosophy that he had begun at Harvard, but most important, learned the fundamentals of modern sociology from the lectures of Professor Georg Simmel that he attended at the university. Locke also studied the works of Professor Gustav Schmoller, who was sympathetic to the Social Democratic movement in Germany. It was in Germany that Locke was more thoroughly exposed to the techniques and ideology of modern sociology and to the concept of class conflict that emerged in his later lectures. Under the influence of these German social scientists, Locke moved away from the notion that social groupings were derivative of human nature to the notion that races and nationalities are products of social forces. Europe also stimulated his appetite for the study of race contacts when London hosted the first Universal Race Congress in July 1911. Locke appears to have attended; he cited Franz Boas and Felix von Luschan, who lectured at the conference, in *Race Contacts*.[41]

Although Locke traveled in eastern Europe, where he observed some of the European ethnic conflict he discussed in lecture 4, he was unable to finance a research trip through Europe, Africa, and the Middle East to study race contacts. Lacking an income in Europe, Locke returned to the United States in 1911 and began to build his reputation as a black spokesperson. In "The Negro and a Race Tradition" (1911), a public lecture delivered to both the American Negro Historical Society in Philadelphia and the Yonkers Negro Society for Historical Research in New York, he recommended that blacks develop a race consciousness based on their cultural ties with African civilization. As he stated later in lecture 5 of *Race Contacts*, blacks had a right to a cultural sense of belongingness that extended to all of the black diaspora; they should not sacrifice that right in the struggle to win acceptance in white America.[42] By calling for a race consciousness among blacks, Locke worked within lines of reasoning well established among educated blacks. Certainly, John Edward Bruce, cofounder of the Yonkers Society and an elder statesman of American black nationalism, found Locke's views consistent with his own.[43] Du Bois had urged race consciousness in his American Negro Academy address, "The Conservation of the Races," as early as 1897. But Locke was much more skeptical about the permanency of race differences or the presence of race consciousness in the black population than either Du Bois or Bruce. Locke's advocacy of the race ideal was an accommodation to his African American audience: he knew his comparative perspective on race attitudes would not be popular, but advocacy of race loyalty would. In the words of Arthur Fauset, Locke's friend and colleague, "Locke made himself into an Africanist."[44] Like a good pragmatist, Locke voiced the sentiment of raciality as the key to black advancement in America: blacks must use the myth of race to promote their development, just as nineteenth-century Europeans had used it to promote their own.

Moreover, his ideology of race consciousness was quite consistent with Booker T. Washington's conservative plan for black self-development under segregation. This was no accident: he was professionally indebted to Washington as well as intellectually sympathetic to the program of the "sage of Tuskegee." Washington had given his blessing to Locke's comparative study of race contacts in 1910 and then had invited the Rhodes Scholar to accompany him on a train trip through Florida in the summer of 1912. Through Washington's intercession, Locke secured his position at Howard University in the fall of that year. Locke praised Washington's leadership role in the black community but also began to realize, especially after his abortive attempt to return to Germany in 1914, that he needed a more comprehensive ideology. Washington's faith that black self-development could flourish under segregation was challenged by Locke's growing understanding, gained in Europe, that blacks would be severely constricted by imperialism, capitalism, and racism even if they achieved the maximum progress possible under segregation.[45]

He returned from Europe in the fall of 1914 to articulate more forcefully his critical feelings about imperialism and race practice. In "The Great Disillusionment," another address before the Yonkers Society on September 26, Locke argued that World War I was a race war, which had broken out between two arms of Anglo-Saxon civilization, England and Germany, over the spoils of empire.[46] Locke was the first African American to argue that imperialism caused the war (a position on which W. E. B. Du Bois would elaborate in more detail in his *Atlantic Monthly* article, "The African Roots of the War," eight months later).[47] But Locke's most important point was that the war destroyed the ideological justification of imperialism, that is, that imperialism was necessary because it brought a morally superior Anglo-Saxon civilization to "barbaric" peoples. The war proved that the Europeans were just as barbaric, if not more so, than those they had colonized. Rather than a history of unlimited progress, as Social Darwinists had claimed, the story of Anglo-Saxon imperialism was now revealed for what it was—a greedy grab for wealth and power. No longer could a European nation claim it had a divine right to rule, and no longer did peoples of color owe the West any allegiance for its supposed moral and cultural superiority. He urged his listeners to view their distance from European culture as an asset rather than a liability.

After "The Great Disillusionment," Locke renewed efforts to gain approval for the *Race Contacts* lecture series by Howard University. Originally, he had begun drafting the lectures in the spring of 1914, but only succeeded in giving them in April and May of 1915 after students of the NAACP campus chapter and Deans Miller of the College of Arts and Sciences and Moore of the Teachers College agitated for them.[48] Continued student interest in the lectures enabled him to repeat the series in March and April of 1916, which was a victory. Probably no other school in America would have allowed him publicly to criticize imperialism and missionarism, on the one hand, and racial ideology and segregation, on the other. But Locke never won approval to teach the course as part of the regular curriculum, even when he volunteered to do so without additional compensation.

Why Howard refused to approve Locke's courses on race relations remains a mystery. However, the answer may lie with its president. From its founding in 1867, Howard's presidents had been mostly conservative white ministers who rejected the notion that Howard University was a black institution. The Reverend S. M. Newman, the president in 1916, was particularly discouraging of the idea that Negro or race studies should be developed at Howard. In addition, the American Missionary Association influenced some members of the Howard Board of Trustees, which might explain why Locke apologized in lecture 2 for his view that missionary work was a tool of Western imperialism. Others, such as the young African American Dean Kelly Miller, were enthusiastic and encouraging; even William Sinclair, the Philadelphia physician and board of trustees member, lobbied for Locke's work. But it would be eleven years before Howard University would have its first black president and institutional motivation to develop race studies. In 1916 Locke had to remain content to publish privately his syllabus of the lectures as a pamphlet, after which he took a leave of absence to do graduate work that resulted in a Ph.D. in philosophy from Harvard University.[49]

When Locke returned to Howard in 1917, he found the university had mobilized to train officers for segregated units in the Army. America's entry into the war had unleashed a wave of patriotism that swept both black and white communities. Locke's criticism of the war ceased and, in his address to the Howard University freshman class in 1918, he suggested the aftermath of the war might contain new opportunities for the educated black elite. The war had weakened the authority of older aristocracies, he argued in "The Role of the Talented Tenth," with the result that leadership positions in the future might be filled on the basis of merit and talent, rather than blood and race. Even though Locke had declared earlier that the war was a fight for the spoils of colonialism, he, like Du Bois, hoped that black participation in the effort would be rewarded with freedom for Germany's African colonies and better treatment of Negroes in America.[50] But the Treaty of Versailles, the Red Scare, and the violent Red Summer of 1919 dashed these hopes. The Allies refused to extend President Wilson's principle of self-determination to Germany's African colonies; instead, the Allies divided them among themselves. The Bolshevik Revolution in Russia in 1917 and the Third International's 1919 call for workers to seize power around the world frightened the U. S. government. When bombs exploded at the homes of government officials in the spring of 1919, many Americans reacted hysterically and supported the ensuing anti-communist campaign to root out the internal enemy. Anyone expressing unconventional opinions was persecuted as a revolutionary. That summer, gangs of white youths and ex-servicemen attacked blacks in American cities, especially those cities that had experienced large immigrations of black people during the war. In Washington, an irresponsible publicity campaign by the *Washington Post* sparked several days of rioting, during which blacks fought back with unexpected ferocity. Washington remained divided into armed camps for almost two weeks, and in the aftermath of the riot, race antipathies and prejudice hardened.[51]

Not surprisingly, Locke, by now a middle-aged professor at Howard University, ceased public discussion of the radical aspects of his theory of race in the aftermath of the war and rioting. At age thirty-five in 1920, Locke had reached the "settling-down age," as Daniel Levinson, the social psychologist describes it.[52] To be a radical would have committed Locke to a vagabond life: there was little future for him at Howard or any other black school in the 1920s if he continued to stress a theory that emphasized the persistence of race and class conflict in a modern capitalist state. There were limits to how critical Locke felt he could be and still perform the role of a black educator. Locke decided to leave radicalism to the students he taught, although even this strategy did not prevent him from getting into trouble: in 1925 he was dismissed from Howard when his support for a fair faculty pay scale and for student demands to end compulsory chapel and ROTC led him to be branded a malcontent by Howard's white president, J. Stanley Durkee. Fortunately, Locke was able to earn a living as an author and a lecturer of the New Negro Renaissance, until 1927, when he was reinstated by the new black president of Howard, Mordecai Johnson.[53]

But Locke had gotten the message by 1919: so completely did he drop his critique of American racism that he did not publish anything of significance between 1919 and 1922. Indeed, as Arnold Rampersad has suggested, Locke entered the black literary scene of the 1920s without a clear professional identity: he had not carved out a sphere of research as W. E. B. Du Bois had done.[54] In fact, however, unknown to others Locke had defined a research area. What Locke did in the 1920s was to shift gears professionally, to deemphasize the controversial political and sociological side of his theory, and put into practice the aesthetic program he had outlined in lecture 5 of *Race Contacts*—that African Americans should develop a race consciousness based on black art and literature. When a critical mass of black writers began to emerge, Locke wrote a series of articles on contemporary black literature that culminated in "Harlem: Mecca of the New Negro," a special issue of the *Survey Graphic* magazine, published on 1 March 1925, that contained Locke's essays, along with poems, short stories, and essays by black writers of the 1920s. Locke would follow that immensely successful issue, which he had also edited, with a book-length anthology, *The New Negro: An Interpretation*, published in December 1925. By writing about Harlem and the New Negro, Locke found a public identity as the spokesperson of the New Negro literary movement of the 1920s.[55]

The quickening of literary activity among blacks in the mid-1920s was, of course, consistent with Locke's earlier recommendation that blacks develop a race consciousness. "Each generation," he wrote in the *Survey Graphic* essay, "Enter the New Negro," "will have its creed and that of the present is the belief in the efficacy of collective effort, in race cooperation. This deep feeling of race is at present the mainspring of Negro life."[56] Locke reinvoked earlier analogies between European and African American nationalism to explain the significance of Harlem: "Without pretense to their political significance, Harlem has the same role to play for the New Negro as Dublin has had for the New Ireland or Prague for the New Czechoslovakia."[57] Although Locke did not abandon his Hegelian expectation that this "secondary race consciousness" would ultimately be merged into the "general civilization type," his cultural advocacy of the 1920s emphasized the kind of race nationalism in black literature and culture that he had outlined in lecture 5 of *Race Contacts*.

In pushing the practical implications of his theory into the forefront, Locke did not completely jettison the insights of the rest of *Race Contacts*: rather, those perceptions about American race practice undergirded his more literary positions. Like a good social historian, Locke credited the Great Migration of poor blacks into the urban North as the most important factor in the intellectual change of black life: it was the masses who were "leading and the leaders who are following."[58] Similarly, he dismissed the fiction of segregation that "the life of the races is separate" and rejected the notion that the missionary-like philanthropy of white-black relations could be perpetuated in the modern era.[59] He reassured his audience that this new movement was not separatist; instead, it was "a constructive effort to build the obstructions in the stream of his progress into an efficient dam of social energy and power."[60] Ideas continued to follow social practice, as Locke's earlier scientific analysis of race had predicted. The changed social conditions of black life had produced a New Negro, who was now on the verge of a true self-consciousness: "Hitherto it must be admitted that American Negroes have been a race more in name than in fact, or to be exact, more in sentiment than in experience. The chief bond between them has been a common condition rather than a common consciousness; a problem in common rather than a life in common. In Harlem, Negro life is seizing upon its first chances for group expression and self-determination."[61]

Indeed, the New Negro image was only the most recent of literary images that changed over time and reflected the alteration in the social conditions of black life in America. In "The American Literary Tradition and the Negro" (1926), Locke utilized this theory of the changing nature of racial attitudes to offer one of the first outlines of the changing image of blacks in American literature.[62] Sensing what later historians would document, that the earliest encounter with Africans reflected more an attitude of strangeness than racial repression, Locke charted the shifting images of blacks in American literature as a road map to the functions Africans and later African Americans performed in southern and northern societies.[63] No monolithic stereotype, the black image had changed dramatically from the colonial to the postbellum periods, and would certainly change again after the New Negro period. Now the contemporary period promised that African Americans could begin to define their own image through literary productivity.

Despite Locke's literary pursuits, he continued to follow developments in anthropology and race scholarship, and found time to publish articles in the 1920s that echoed concerns he had voiced in 1916. His 1923 review of Roland Dixon's *The Racial History of Man* reiterated his criticisms of pseudoscientific studies that crudely attributed cultural accomplishments of groups to their physical characteristics.[64] His 1924 article "The Concept of Race as Applied to Social Culture" renewed the argument that environment and not heredity was the cause of perceivable differences between groups.[65] But "The Concept of Race as Applied to Social Culture," published in *The Howard Review*, did not revive his earlier analysis that such false conceptions of race were fueled by the practice of European imperialism.

Instead, Locke developed the cultural side of his theory of race in the 1920s—that race had a cultural basis, that culturally created differences between groups existed, and that such differences could be recognized without capitulating to racists. Locke could then argue that three hundred years of American history had produced a distinctive African American culture that was itself undergoing change. In the 1920s he sought to bring others around to this position. For example, Locke enlisted Melville Herskovits, a Franz Boas student and a prolific critic of pseudoscientific racists, in his effort to bring scholarly recognition to the idea that a distinctive black culture existed in America. Initially, the attempt backfired: when Locke asked Herskovits to document the distinctive cultural life-style of Harlem blacks for the special Harlem issue of *Survey Graphic*, Herskovits stated in his article that he could see no difference between black and white New Yorkers. Although Locke disagreed with this position, he published the article anyway and continued to discuss the issue with Herskovits. Historian Walter A. Jackson credits such discussions with Locke (and others) with moving Herskovits away from his stark assimilationist position toward an appreciation for African American distinctiveness and a desire to research the persistence of African influences in black American life and culture.[66] Eventually, Herskovits published "The Negro in the New World" in 1930 and his magnum opus, *The Myth of the Negro Past*, in 1941, which argued for the survival of African cultural forms, even in Harlem.[67]

Locke's own seminal contribution to this debate came in 1928, when he published "The Negro's Contribution to American Art and Literature."[68] Like Herskovits's later work, Locke's essay credited Africa as the source of the "basic imaginative background" of African American creativity. But like Guy Johnson in *Folk Culture on St. Helena Island, South Carolina* (1930), Locke emphasized how completely African and Anglo-American cultures had been syncretized in African American folk culture, although Locke gave more credit to African cultural survivals than did Johnson.[69] Even more provocatively, Locke suggested that much of southern culture was African American and thus symbolic of a kind of cultural victory over the European American: "It is just as important, perhaps more so, to color the humor of a country, or to influence its tempo of life and feeling, or to mould its popular song, dance and folktale, as it is to affect its formal poetry or art or music."[70] Having called for a greater African American contribution to American culture in 1911, Locke recorded his recognition in 1928 that such a contribution on the folk level had already occurred. Much of Locke's earlier theory made it possible for him to be flexible as a spokesperson not only for the Negro Renaissance, but also for the view that social change was leading inevitably to greater integration and cultural blending in America.

But Locke's ascendancy in cosmopolitan literary circles came at a price. Committed as a publicist of the Renaissance to write for a popular audience and to garner white support for the fledgling movement, he left out the hard-nosed criticism of white paternalism and the revealing analogies between race and class conflict that had peppered his earlier work. Locke seemed to fall into doing a history of race contacts rather than a scientific examination of their contemporary operation. Even worse, some of Locke's articles, such as "The Negro's Contribution to American Art and Literature," seemed to lend credence to the notion that blacks possessed an intrinsic artistic nature. To account for the particular aesthetic creativity of black Americans, he argued that "it was the African or racial temperament, creeping back in the overtones of his half-articulate speech and action, which gave to his life and ways the characteristic qualities instantly recognized as peculiarly and representatively his."[71] Locke's movement away from criticism of white paternalism and toward an essentialist view of racial character may have been influenced by his increasing dependence in the late 1920s on the financial support of Charlotte Mason, a white millionaire, who, in addition to being a fierce anti-Marxist, also believed that blacks and Indians were noble primitives who could reform Western civilization.[72] Perhaps buoyed by the attention he gained as a spokesperson and encouraged by the financial support he received for his artistic projects, Locke abandoned the skeptical disinterestedness of his earlier lectures for increasingly optimistic predictions of the future benefits of this new cultural appreciation from whites. During the 1930s, as conditions worsened for blacks in the midst of the Great Depression, Locke would come under criticism, somewhat unfairly, for having argued that art and literature would liberate black people from white oppression.[73]

Moreover, Locke could not long maintain the precious equipoise of *The New Negro* between race consciousness and the promise of integration into the American middle class. Dedicated to striking a balance between the desire of black writers for access to the mainstream and the need of black people for a race tradition, he found that such artists as Countee Cullen, Claude McKay, and Wallace Thurman rebelled against his brand of racial idealism.[74] As some writers turned to writing Harlem nightlife stories almost exclusively, the serious connections with political self-determination Locke had hoped to maintain all but evaporated.[75] Compared with the political nationalism advanced by Marcus Garvey in the early 1920s, Locke's New Negro arts movement must have seemed a relief to educated whites. Even his call for broader recognition of African American folk culture was a relatively benign recommendation for a black intellectual of the 1920s. It was certainly not as threatening as a direct critique of segregation and its economic and political underpinnings. Bereft of the political anger and sociological criticism of *Race Contacts*, Locke's writings of the late 1920s lost some of their edge.

When political opinion shifted to the left in the 1930s, Locke began to resuscitate his earlier analysis of race. But first he was criticized by such younger black social scientists as Abram Harris, Ralph Bunche, and E. Franklin Frazier at Howard University, who, inspired by Marxism, shifted the African American debate from race to class, and from middle-class discrimination to the problems of the black working class. Indeed, many of these Young Turks, as historian James Young has called them, viewed the emphasis on race in the writings of black intellectuals as an obstacle to the kind of interracial working class unity they believed essential for changing the American situation.[76] Unaware of Locke's earlier lectures on race, the Young Turks generally regarded Locke as a misguided proponent of racial art. But Locke's theory helped him to sympathize with the new Marxist analysis and to move from a racial to an integrationist aesthetic. Given his belief that the racial climate of opinion shifted over time, Locke rationalized his changing views as a natural evolution. With a fundamental theory that accommodated racialist and integrationist observations within it, Locke could shift with the dialectical winds of race practice in America. Thus, when he founded the publishing company The Associates in Negro Folk Education in the 1930s, he published Ralph Bunche's Marxist critique of race, *A World View of Race*, in a series.[77] Although he believed Bunche overstated the case that race was not a factor in modern life, Locke supported Bunche's efforts and published his work. Locke encouraged this new generation of historians, economists, and sociologists in his retrospective reviews for *Opportunity* magazine during the 1930s, even though he cautioned them to appreciate the influence of race and culture if they wished to understand truly the situation of minorities in America and the colonial world.[78] Like other social scientists, Marxists need a concept of race and a concept of culture, just as modern anthropologists need an understanding of the global, political, and economic context of contemporary culture contact.

Locke elaborated on these insights when he finally published his theory of race and imperialism in *When Peoples Meet: A Study in Race and*

Culture Contacts (1942) with Bernhard Stern.[79] In the chapter introductions of this reader in anthropology, Locke used his theory of race to elucidate the discussion of world imperialism. The distinguishing characteristic of this book was, as E. Franklin Frazier himself acknowledged, "that it avoided the tendency of some authors to view culture as something abstracted from economic interests, and the opposite tendency of other authors to view problems of race and culture contact as solely economic phenomena."[80] In effect, Locke was a harmonizer between the Marxist and cultural pluralist perspectives on race. Unfortunately, Locke's commentary on these issues remained brief in *When Peoples Meet*; he merely updated his earlier analysis from 1916. And he did not expand his theory of race into a full-length monograph on the subject. His concept of the historical phenomenon of race did shape the analysis of "The Negro in the Three Americas," a lecture series he delivered in Haiti in 1943.[81] Here he sought to integrate the notion that New World slave societies were settled under different social and economic conditions with an analysis of how differences between Latin and Anglo-Saxon cultures shaped New World societies. Locke appears to have been working on a synthesis of his cultural and sociological analyses in the study of black people in North American culture when he died in 1954.[82]

In the end, Locke felt most comfortable with the idea that cultural pluralism was the most accurate "rationalization" of his life and work.[83] Cultural pluralism better served his purpose as a platform of constructive action than his critique of the world system of imperialism. For Locke, the arts projected a healthier image of black identity and capabilities than the harsher view of black life presented by political and sociological perspectives. In choosing to emphasize art and race consciousness over the social sciences and Marxism in his professional life, Locke had creatively answered the question that dogged most black American intellectuals of the early twentieth century: in the face of vicious and unyielding white racism, "What could the Negro do?"

Contemporary Relevance

No contemporary thinker has blended together in one statement or theory the many diverse insights Locke offers in *Race Contacts*. Perhaps this is because it is impossible to reconcile satisfactorily all the conflicting perspectives in Locke's theory. Certainly, Locke does not seem to have done so. But rather remarkably, much of what Locke said in 1916 has become accepted by historians, sociologists, and anthropologists over the past thirty years. Many of his insights have become integrated into the body of educated thinking on race in America. Perhaps most important has been the decline—shall we hope extinction—of the belief in the social relevance of the biological sense of race, and with that, correspondingly, a rather complete acceptance of the cultural idea of race. Indeed, except in those areas where race is used to define a medical population, that is, a group of people defined by their heightened susceptibility to certain diseases, race as a biological construct has been thoroughly discredited.

But Locke's most important insight was that race relations change and pass through definitive stages or phases in relation to political, economic, and demographic change in society. In *The Origins of the New South* (1951) and *The Strange Career of Jim Crow* (1955), C. Vann Woodward used a similar argument to answer those who saw race as the central theme of Southern history.[84] Without knowing it, Woodward followed in Locke's footsteps when he observed that segregation was a new stage in Southern race relations and not the automatic outcome of slavery, that racial feelings intensified with the sudden removal of formal barriers (emancipation), and that a class and power conflict between whites (the Populist Revolt) was the cause of the turn towards segregation and Negrophobia in the South at the end of the nineteenth century. The argument of Woodward's student, J. Morgan Kousser, that the installation of disfranchisement during the Populist era was proposed mainly by the elite, confirms another of Locke's insights—that race feelings are not automatic, but cultivated deliberately by elites to maintain political control.[85] These historians have substantiated what Locke proposed theoretically in 1916—that racism changes over time. Perhaps Locke's work will encourage further investigation into how and why race feelings react to changes in American social relations.

Essential to this line of historical inquiry is the insight Locke advanced in 1916 that racial conflict is not primarily a response to the color or culture of a targeted group, but rather the result of economic and political competition for survival and status in competitive societies. This view of American racism was outlined in Oliver Cox's classic study, *Caste, Class and Race* (1948), which argued that economic processes were more important than racial and cultural differences in causing American race conflict.[86] The cause of race conflict, Cox suggested, was not color but ethnic competition between different class groups. More recently this view has been elaborated into a split-labor market theory by sociologist Edna Bonacich, who argues that most ethnic antagonism arises when one group can sell its labor cheaper than another group, and that other group has the resources to fight back with violence or other "caste-like measures."[87] Such an analysis tends to move the discussion of race relations away from a focus on the concept of race and toward the idea that race is merely the battleground of largely class-based interests.

Locke's insight that race is essentially an ideology that masks other interests has also become increasingly popular of late with intellectual historians of race in America. Whereas Winthrop Jordan, in his classic study, *White Over Black* (1971), analyzed racism as a psychological reaction to color and a permanent feature of black-white relations, more recent studies, such as David Brion Davis's *The Problem of Slavery in the Age of Revolution, 1770–1823* (1975), have approached race as a vortex in which issues range from the possibilities of moral perfectionism to the problem of discipline of forced laborers, white and black.[88] Davis's work suggests that fears about the aftermath of emancipation were driven as much by the moral problem of coercion in a so-called free society as by fear of contamination by "untouchables." Locke's voice can be heard here as well: race is most often the way multiracial societies resolve conflicts over power and labor that are not primarily racial concerns.

What distinguishes Locke's work from some of this recent historiography is his unwillingness to jettison the concept of race once it has been demystified. Several studies of the South, such as Steven Hahn's *The Roots of Southern Populism* (1983), Jonathan Wiener's *Social Origins of the New South* (1978), and Jay Mandle's *The Roots of Black Poverty* (1978), reduce racism to being nothing more than class consciousness.[89] The implication is that even avowed Southern racists were not motivated by racial feelings, but by unacknowledged (and perhaps unconscious) class reactions. More subtly, Barbara Fields, in her festschrift essay, "Race and Ideology in American History," has acknowledged the power of racial ideology even as she has described race as subordinate to class in understanding American history.[90] Locke would agree that race is often disguised class conflict; but he also argued that once class issues have been transformed into racial concerns, the latter often have more emotional power than class feelings alone. For Locke, not only does the

1

concept of race grip the modern mind too tightly to be dispensed with, but also racial ideas are stirred by a practice of racial discrimination grounded in political as well as economic struggle. Moreover, although class may be the ultimate cause, race is often how colonized peoples experience exploitation—an insight put to telling use in *The Highest Stage of White Supremacy* (1985), John Cell's comparative study of segregation in the American South and South Africa.[91] As Cell writes, "Racism is indeed what Lenin called false consciousness. It is nonetheless real and powerful."[92] In this schema, race as a category may be used as a metaphor for group power: just as class defines one's relationship to the means of production and hence one's access to economic power, so race may effectively define one's relationship to a group, whose changing size, resources, and reputation affect one's life experiences.

Indeed, some historians and sociologists who accept the economic aspects of race conflict nevertheless are beginning to argue that race remains a useful concept, because it describes aspects of human reaction that are not completely accounted for in a strictly Marxist analysis. In *Race Relations in Sociological Theory* (1970), for example, John Rex argues that the victims of colonialism are in a different relationship to the bourgeoisie than the white working class.[93] Those on the periphery of the world system of capitalism stand in a different relationship to world imperialism than those at its metropolitan center. Rex also notices something Locke described in *Race Contacts*: the treatment of peoples of color is quite different on the frontier, that is in South Africa, than it is in Europe—the case of East Indian laborers in England. As was Locke, Rex is open to the notion that cultural issues play a role in the behavior of groups toward one another in an economically charged situation. And Rex retains belief in the primacy of class in race conflict: "It is not solely because of the bonds of ethnicity that, say, East Indians in Guyana remain a distinct group, but because men united in this way have been assigned a particular role in the economic, political and legal order."[94] Where Rex diverges is in his insistence that racial conflict is different in kind from ethnic conflict. Rex labels as racism only that conflict that has an explicit or implicit theoretical justification on racial grounds (what Locke called a "race creed"). Locke's conception was broader: the root of racism was in its *practice*, not in its theoretical justification, which was characteristic only of its modern form.

Locke's lectures are also relevant to the current debate over the role of culture in social relations. One of the most interesting perspectives on

li

this cultural dimension of race appears in an essay by J. William Harris, a professor of history at the University of New Hampshire, who has also suggested that race can be most profitably viewed as a cultural system that serves some as yet undetermined function in American society.[95] His work supports Locke's suggestions in lecture 3 of *Race Contacts* and later in "American Literary Tradition and the Negro" and "The Negro in the Three Americas" that an integration of the insights of sociology and culture may hold the answer to why racism persists even when it does not serve the economic interests of those who practice it. Such a perspective helps direct our attention to the largely unconscious set of rules, reflexes, and attitudes that dictate the social etiquette of race relations.

Locke harnessed in one theory what are often regarded today as two mutually exclusive positions: one, that race relations are merely a subset of a more comprehensive set of problems confronting modern society, and two, that a distinctive African American culture exists that should be studied and promoted in order to enhance African-American identity and group power. In terms of the latter, probably the best contemporary expression of Locke's social view of the origins of black culture can be found in Houston A. Baker, Jr.'s *Blues, Ideology, and Afro-American Literature: A Vernacular Theory* (1984), which defines a blues aesthetic that is grounded not in biological genealogy but in the material conditions of the black experience of America.[96] Baker has produced a synthesis of elements contained in Locke's *Race Contacts* and *The New Negro*: the social history of the black experience of America has crystallized into a distinctive vernacular culture that now shapes the symbol systems of black and white American discourse. Similarly, Locke's notion of a modernist black culture is alive in the art criticism of Richard Powell, whose catalogue to the exhibition *The Blues Aesthetic: Black Culture and Modernism* (1989) examines black culture in terms of a blues aesthetic that is available to both black and white artists.[97]

But the blending of a materialist and a culturally pluralist vision of the African American presence in American society is Locke's distinctive contribution, a reflection perhaps of the disciplinary union of sociology and art in his theory. His achievement is all the more remarkable because a division in approach has existed between sociological and aesthetic perspectives on race: that split has characterized those who have theorized about race in American intellectual history. That split has also reflected a difference of opinion between those assimilationists, whether Marxist or conservative, who believe that race is best down-played in American life and those cultural nationalists who believe that race remains an important tool for the liberation of the black commu-nity. But for Locke, race is not simply a tool for understanding the black community, but also a tool for understanding the American identity. For it is precisely the promise of American life that a new race—or what Locke would call the "civilization type"—called the American would emerge out of the blending of immigrant races. While race has often implied a politics of divisiveness and disunity, Locke finds in the poetics of race a unifying force: not the "melting pot," but the diversity of cultures persisting in harmony is the promise of American democracy for Locke. Race becomes not only a tool for empowering African Amer-icans, but also a tool for understanding the highest aspirations and potentials of the American character. Race is a constitutive force of the American identity.

Locke may have also balanced contrary views of race on one intellec-tual beam because as a black intellectual in 1916 he felt compelled to articulate both a theoretical and a practical perspective on race. On a practical level, race was the experienced reality of a black intellectual living in the segregated American world of 1916. He may have felt that something, anything, had to be tried to allow for the practical survival of blacks. Some may argue that race has become anachronistic in the 1990s when segregation has been repudiated, at least ideologically. Yet, as a social observer, Locke remains prophetic: his notion that race and ethnic consciousness would recur and persist has been borne out both in the United States and in the Soviet Union of the 1990s, to pick only two examples. The resurgence of anti-Semitism and Baltic nationalism in the Soviet Union and of racism and black consciousness on college campuses in the United States is occurring at a time of changing eco-nomic conditions, most notably the deepening of a world-wide reces-sion. Even more pointedly, chronically unemployed skinheads in the recently unified Germany have violently attacked African emigrant workers under the guise of keeping the German identity pure. Increas-ing competition for scarce resources will stimulate the search for scape-goats by displaced classes and entrenched elites who find themselves challenged from within and without. Since the political benefits of encouraging conflict often outweigh the rewards of corrective social change, it seems likely that race baiting and provocation will continue. Yet even as we seem to enter what appears to be a new phase of race relations, we should keep in mind Locke's advice not to elevate the phenomena of race into laws. Observing the contemporary scene in this country, Locke might still conclude, as he did at the end of lecture 3, that "we shall have to come [to a] position in race problems [analysis where we] regard some of the reactions of our present situation in America as indicative of a final stage, and welcome them as such, because they seem to be born of the very last effort of society to stem the inevitable when they confront [the reality of progressive change.] But, of course[,] they can only have that sense of jeopardy when they are confronted by an apparent and what may be an actual realization that the fetish of the distinctions is about the only thing that is left." Let us hope so.

NOTES

1. Alain Locke to Mary Locke, 23 March 1916, Alain Locke Papers, Moorland-Spingarn Research Center, Howard University. Hereafter referred to as "ALP, HU." *Howard University Catalogue, 1912–13* vol. 7, no. 2 (March 1913); William A. Sinclair to Rev. S. M. Newman, President of Howard University, 18 September 1915, ALP, HU.

2. President of the Howard Chapter of the NAACP to the board of deans at Howard University, 18 April 1914, ALP, HU.

3. Alain Locke, Memorandum Re: Negro-Americana, 3 February 1915, ALP, HU.

4. Rayford W. Logan, *Howard University: The First Hundred Years, 1867–1967* (New York: New York University Press, 1969), 171.

5. Card Announcement, "A Course of Lectures under the auspices of The Howard Chapter of the N.A.A.C.P. The Social Science Club, The Teachers and the Commercial Colleges, on RACE CONTACTS AND INTER-RACIAL RELATIONS A study of the Theory and Practice of Race. BY PROFESSOR ALAIN LEROY LOCKE, A.B., B. LITT." ALP, HU.

6. Alain Locke to Mary Locke, n.d., ALP, HU.

7. Thomas F. Gossett, *Race: The History of an Idea in America* (Dallas: Southern Methodist University Press, 1963), 263– 80, 292, 340; George Fredrickson, *The Black Image in the White Mind: The Debate on Afro-American Character and Destiny, 1817–1914* (New York: Harper, 1972), 256–82; William J. Tuttle, *Race Riot: Chicago in the Red Summer of 1919* (New York: Atheneum, 1970), 5–13; Constance M. Green, *The Secret City* (Princeton, N.J.: Princeton University Press, 1967), 77–78, 190–93.

8. Joseph Arthur Comte de Gobineau, *Essai sur l'inégalité des races humaines* (4 vols. Paris: Didot, 1853–55); abridged English edition, *The Moral and Intellectual Diversity of Races, with Particular Reference to Their Respective Influence in the Civil and Political History of Mankind* (Philadelphia: Lippincott, 1856); another abridged edition, *The Inequality of Human Races*, trans. by Adrian Collins, with an introduction by Dr. Oscar Levy (New York: G.P. Putnam & Sons, 1915); Gossett, *Race*, 342–47, 281–83; Fredrickson, *Black Image in the White Mind*, 249–55.

9. Fredrickson, *Black Image in the White Mind*, 312–19; Gossett, *Race*, 167–75.

10. William Toll, *The Resurgence of Race: Black Social Theory from Reconstruction to the Pan African Conferences* (Philadelphia: Temple University Press, 1979), 29–38.

11. Toll, *Resurgence of Race*, 38–46, 139.

12. W. E. B. Du Bois, "The Conservation of Races," American Negro Academy, *Occasional Papers*, No. 2 (1897); reprinted in *W. E. B. Du Bois Writings* (New York: The Library of America, 1986), 815–26.

13. Ibid., 815.

14. Ibid., 817.

15. Franz Boas, "Instability of Human Types" in *Inter-Racial Problems: Papers from the First Universal Races Congress Held in London in 1911*, ed. by G. Spiller, with a new introduction by Herbert Aptheker (New York: Citadel Press, 1970; orig. pub. 1911), 99–108; Boas, "Changes in the Bodily Form of Descendants of Immigrants, 1910–13," in *Race, Language and Culture* (New York: Macmillan, 1949), 63–72; Boas, *The Mind of Primitive Man*, rev. ed. with a new introduction by Melville Herskovits (New York: Collier Books, 1963; orig. pub. 1911); George W. Stocking, Jr., "Franz Boas and the Culture Concept in Historical Perspective," in *Race, Culture, and Evolution: Essays in the History of Anthropology* (New York: The Free Press, 1968), 195–233.

16. Gossett, *Race*, 286.

17. Ruth Benedict, *Patterns of Culture* (Boston: Houghton Mifflin, 1934).

18. See Boas's "Human Faculty as Determined by Race" and "Psychological Problems in Anthropology" in *The Shaping of American Anthropology, 1883–1911*, ed. by George W. Stocking, Jr. (New York: Basic Books, 1974), 221–54; also see Stocking's headnote, "Racial Capacity and Cultural Determinism," 219–20.

19. Franz Boas, *Race and Democratic Society* (New York: J.J. Augustin, 1945), 20–27, 80–81. "Thus it would seem that man being what he is, the Negro problem will not disappear in America until the Negro blood has been so much diluted that it will no longer be recognized just as anti-Semitism will not disappear until the last vestige of the Jew as a Jew has disappeared." (p. 81)

20. Immanuel Wallerstein, *The Modern World-System: Capitalist Agriculture and the Origins of the European World-Economy in the Sixteenth Century* (New York: Academic Press, 1974).

21. Karl Marx, *Capital, Volume One*, in *The Marx-Engels Reader* 2d. ed., ed. by Robert C. Tucker (New York: W. W. Norton & Co., 1978), 365.

22. Vladimir I. Lenin, *Imperialism: The Last Stage of Capitalism* (Moscow: Foreign Languages Publishing House, 1917). Also see Lenin's "Preliminary Draft Theses on the National and Colonial Questions" (presented to the Second Congress of the Communist International, 5 June 1920) in *Selections from V. I. Lenin and J. V. Stalin on National Colonial Question* (Calcutta: Calcutta Book House, 1975), 56–61.

23. Clifford Geertz, "Ideology as a Cultural System," in *Ideology and Discontent* ed. by David Apter (London: Free Press of Glencoe, 1964), 52–57, 63–65. Geertz provides an excellent examination of "interest" and "strain" theories of ideology as well as an incisive analysis of the role of ideologies as a means of building political consciousness.

24. Madison Grant, *The Passing of the Great Race, or The Racial Basis of European History* (New York: Scribner, 1916).

25. Isaiah Berlin, *Vico & Herder: Two Studies in the History of Ideas* (New York: Vintage Books, 1976), 153–60.

26. See Eugene Genovese, *Roll, Jordan, Roll: The World the Slaves Made* (New York: Random House, 1976).

27. See William James, *Pragmatism: A New Name for Some Old Ways of Thinking* (New York: Longman's Green and Co., 1947; orig. pub. 1907) and *A Pluralistic Universe* (New York: Longman's Green and Co., 1948; orig. pub. 1911).

28. James, "The Moral Equivalent of War" in *The Writings of William James: A Comprehensive Edition* ed. with an introduction by John J. McDermott (New York: The Modern Library, 1968), 660–71.

29. Montgomery Gregory to Alain Locke, Thursday noon, *ca.* 1916, ALP, HU.

30. Toll, *Race*, 193–94.

31. Alain Locke to Mary Locke, 19 March 1916, ALP, HU.

32. Remarks made at the close of discussion on an earlier version of this paper presented on 28 December 1978 at the annual meeting of the American Historical Association.

33. Erik Erikson, *Young Man Luther: A Study in Psychoanalysis and History* (New York: Norton, 1962), 40–47; Erikson, *Life History and the Historical Moment* (New York: Norton, 1975), 18–21, 25–32.

34. John A. Sanders, *100 Years After Emancipation: History of the Philadelphia Negro, 1787–1963* (Philadelphia: privately printed, 1964), 37–41; Alain Locke [autobiographical sketch] in *Twentieth Century Authors: A Biographical Dictionary of Modern Literature*, ed. by Stanley Kunitz and Howard Haycroft (New York: H. H. Wilson Co., 1942), 837.

35. Black Victorian is the appellation I use to refer to those members of the black American middle class in the nineteenth and early twentieth centuries who believed that aggressive assimilation of Victorian manners and social values would improve their position in American life. Willard B. Gatewood, among others, has referred to this class as "aristocrats": see *Aristocrats of Color: The Black Elite 1880–1920* (Bloomington: Indiana University Press, 1991). I have preferred the name Black Victorian to emphasize that, in the absence of a true aristocracy's inheritance of blood lineage and private property, the black bourgeoisie relied on acquiring the cultural symbols of the elite, which, as a strategy, was not unlike that of the Anglo-American bourgeoisie. What distinguishes the Black Victorians is that they used Victorianism—specifically, gentlemanly and ladylike behavior, public morality, and, most important, education—as self-defense against racist threats from above and class erosion from below. Aggressive assimilation of elite Anglo-American values became so burdensome for the younger generation of black intellectuals in the early twentieth century that they rebelled and became what Locke called the New Negroes, who attempted to create an alternative image of the black personality in the literary modernism of the Harlem Renaissance. See Jeffrey C. Stewart, "Alain Locke and Georgia Douglas Johnson, Washington Patrons of Afro-American Modernism," *George Washington University Washington Studies*, No. 12 (July 1986):37–44. For more on Black Victorians, see William D. Peirsen, *Black Yankees: The Development of an Afro-American Subculture in Eighteenth Century New England* (Amherst: University of Massachusetts Press, 1988) and Gilbert Ware, *William Hastie: Grace Under Pressure* (London: Oxford University Press, 1984). Emma Jones Lapsansky's article, "'Since They Got Those Separate Churches': Afro-Americans and Racism in Jacksonian Philadelphia", *American Quarterly* 32 (Spring 1980):54–78, is a superb exploration of how the class nature of black Victorian ideology intensified racial feelings and conflict in Jacksonian Philadelphia.

36. Locke, *Twentieth Century Authors*, 837; Alain Locke, [autobiographical sketch] in *American Philosophy Today and Tomorrow* ed. by Horace M. Kallen and Sidney Hook (New York: L. Furman, Inc., 1935), 313.

37. Sarah Schmidt, "A Conversation with Horace Kallen: The Zionist Chapter of His Life," *Reconstructionist* (November 1975):29; Alain Locke, "A Rhodes Scholar Question," unpublished manuscript, ALP, HU; Locke, "Oxford Contrasts," *Independent* 67(15 July 1909):139–42; Locke, *American Philosophy Today and Tomorrow*, 313.

38. See J. Hector St. John de Crevecoeur, *Letters from an American Farmer* (1782) and *Sketches of Eighteenth-Century America*, ed. with an introduction by Albert E. Stone (New York: Penguin Books, 1983), 69–70.

39. Horace M. Kallen, "Alain Locke and Cultural Pluralism," *Journal of Philosophy* 54 (28 February 1957): 122; Jeffrey C. Stewart, "A Biography of Alain Locke: Philosopher of the Harlem Renaissance, 1886–1930" (Ph.D. diss., Yale University, 1979),79–96, 113–16.

40. "List of Twenty-eight Papers Read," *The Oxford Cosmopolitan* 1 (June 1909):17; H. El Alaily, "Modern Egypt," *The Oxford Cosmopolitan* 1 (June 1909):20–22; Har Dayal, "Obstacles to Cosmopolitanism," *The Oxford Cosmopolitan* 1 (June 1909):27–31; Emily C. Brown, *Har Dayal: Hindu Revolutionary and Rationalist* (Tucson: University of Arizona Press, 1975); Peter Walshe, *The Rise of African Nationalism in South Africa: The African National Congress, 1912–1952* (Berkeley: University of California Press, 1971), 13–14.

41. Locke to Booker T. Washington, 16 March 1910, box 912-Ro-1, Booker T. Washington Papers, Library of Congress, Washington, D.C.; De Fonseka to Alain Locke, 2 July 1911, 2 September 1911, and Mary Locke to Alain Locke, 24 July 1911, ALP, HU. Record of Locke's attendance at the University of Berlin; "Schmoller on Class Conflicts in General," a translation of a passage from Schmoller's *Grundriss der allgemeinen Volkswirtschaftslehre* (1904), appeared in the bibliography that followed lecture 3 of the *Syllabus of an Extension Course of Lectures given in the Spring semesters of 1915 and 1916*, reprinted in Jeffrey C. Stewart, ed. *The Critical Temper of Alain Locke: A Selection of His Essays on Art and Culture* (New York: Garland Publishing, Inc., 1983), 410. Franz Boas and Felix von Luschan are discussed in lecture 1, on pages 7–8.

42. Locke, "The Negro and a Race Tradition," speech summarized in *The New York Age*, 14 December 1911.

43. See Ralph L. Crowder, "John Edward Bruce: Pioneer Black Nationalist," *Afro-Americans in New York Life and History* 2, no. 2 (July 1978), "Death of Sir John Edward Bruce, Knight Commander of the Nile," *The Negro World*, 16 August 1924, and Peter Gilbert, ed. *Selected Writings of John Edward Bruce, Militant Black Journalist* (New York: Arno Press and the New York Times, 1971), especially "An Intellectual Battle," 121–24, and "The Importance of Thinking Black," 131–33.

44. Interview with Arthur Fauset, 27 December 1980.

45. Locke to Booker T. Washington, 23 March 1912, 10 August 1912, 16 September 1912, box 458 L-1, Booker T. Washington Papers, Library of Congress, Washington, D.C.

46. John Edward Bruce to Alain Locke, 21 September 1914, ALP, HU.

47. W. E. B. Du Bois, "The African Roots of the War," *The Atlantic Monthly* 115 (May 1915):707–14.

48. President of the Howard Chapter of the NAACP to the Board of Deans at Howard University, 18 April 1914, ALP, HU; Alain Locke to Mary Locke, 28 April 1915, ALP, HU.

49. Alain Locke to Mary Locke, 19 August 1915, ALP, HU; Walter Dyson, *Howard University: The Capstone of Negro Education* (Washington, D.C.: The Graduate School of Howard University, 1941), 301–14; Rayford Logan, *Howard University: The First Hundred Years* (New York: New York University, 1969), 115–16, 171, 176, 184, 189, 214–20, 258; Alain Locke, *Syllabus of an Extension Course of Lectures on Race Contacts and Inter-Racial Relations: A Study in the Theory and Practice of Race* (Washington, D.C., 1916).

50. Locke to Joel Spingarn, 24 May 1919, Joel R. Spingarn Papers, New York Public Library, New York, N. Y.; Montgomery Gregory to Alain Locke, 17 May 1917, ALP, HU; Locke, "The Role of the Talented Tenth," *Howard University Record* 2 (December 1918):15–18; W.E.B. Du Bois, "Editorial," *The Crisis* (November 1914):28–30.

51. William M. Tuttle, Jr., *Race Riot: Chicago in the Red Summer of 1919* (New York: Atheneum, 1970), 5–22; Constance M. Green, *The Secret City: A History of Race Relations in the Nation's Capital* (Princeton: Princeton University Press, 1967), 190–95; James Weinstein, *The Decline of Socialism in America, 1912–1925* (New York: Vintage, 1969), 230–33.

52. Daniel Levinson, et. al., *The Seasons of a Man's Life* (New York: Alfred Knopf, 1978), 139–49.

53. Logan, *Howard*, 171–72; Raymond Wolters, *The New Negro on Campus* (Princeton, N.J.: Princeton University Press, 1975), 84–89, 101–09; Locke to Paul Kellogg, n.d. box

710, Paul Kellogg Papers, Archives of Social Welfare History, University of Minnesota; Henry Williams, *Black Response to the American Left* (Princeton, N.J.: Princeton University Press, 1973), 89–91.

54. Arnold Rampersad, *The Life of Langston Hughes, Volume I: 1902–1941: I, Too, Sing America* (London: Oxford University Press, 1986), 67.

55. "Harlem: Mecca of the New Negro," *Survey Graphic* 53 (1 March 1925); *The New Negro: An Interpretation*, Alain Locke, ed., with book decorations and portraits by Winold Reiss, (New York: Albert and Charles Boni, 1925).

56. Alain Locke, "Enter the New Negro," *Survey Graphic* 53 (1 March 1925): 632–33.

57. Alain Locke, "Harlem," *Survey Graphic* 53 (1 March 1925):630. 26.

58. Ibid.

59. Locke, "Enter the New Negro," 632.

60. Ibid., 633.

61. Locke, *The New Negro*, 7.

62. Locke, "The American Literary Tradition and the Negro," *Modern Quarterly* 3 (May–July 1926):215–22.

63. See Oscar and Mary F. Handlin, "Origins of the Southern Labor System," *William and Mary Quarterly* Third Series, 7 (April 1950):199–222.

64. Locke, "The Problem of Race Classification," *Opportunity* 1 (September 1923): 261–64.

65. Locke, "The Concept of Race as Applied to Social Culture," *Howard Review* 1 (June 1924):290–99.

66. For more information on the Locke-Melville Herskovits relationship, see Walter A. Jackson, "Melville Herskovits and the Search for Afro-American Culture," *History of Anthropology* 4 (1986):78–86.

67. Melville Herskovits, "The Negro in the New World: The Statement of a Problem," (1930) in *The New World Negro* (Bloomington: Indiana University Press, 1966), 1–12; Herskovits, *The Myth of the Negro Past* (New York: Harper & Row, 1941).

68. Locke, "The Negro's Contribution to American Art and Literature," *Annals of the American Academy of Political and Social Science* 140 (November 1928):234–47; reprinted in *The Critical Temper of Alain Locke: A Selection of His Essays on Art and Culture* (New York: Garland Publishing, Inc., 1983), 439–50.

69. Guy B. Johnson, *Folk Culture on St. Helena Island, South Carolina* (Chapel Hill: University of North Carolina Press, 1930); Daniel Joseph Singal, *The War Within: From Victorian to Modernist Thought in the South, 1919–1945* (Chapel Hill: University of North Carolina Press, 1982), 322–24.

70. Locke, "The Negro's Contribution to American Art and Literature," in *The Critical Temper of Alain Locke*, 440.

71. Locke, "The Negro's Contribution," in *The Critical Temper of Alain Locke*, 439.

72. For more information on Mrs. Charlotte Mason, see Stewart, "A Biography of Alain Locke," 323–29.

73. John A. Davis, "We Win the Right to Fight for Jobs," *Opportunity* 16 (August 1938):232; Richard Wright, "Blueprint for Negro Writing," *New Challenge* 2 (Fall 1937):53–65.

74. Nathan Irvin Huggins, *Harlem Renaissance* (New York and Oxford: Oxford University Press, 1971), 205–26; Wallace Thurman, *Infants of the Spring* (New York: Macaulay Co., 1932).

75. Locke to Mrs. Charlotte Mason, 13 September 1931, ALP, HU.

76. James O. Young, *Black Writers of the Thirties* (Baton Rouge: Louisiana State University Press, 1973).

77. Ralph Bunche, *A World View of Race* Bronze Booklet No. 4. (Washington, D.C.: The Associates in Negro Folk Education, 1936).

78. See Alain Locke's "God Save Reality! Retrospective Review of the Literature of the Negro: 1936, Part II," *Opportunity* 15 (February 1937):40–44; "Dry Fields and Green Pastures," *Opportunity* 18 (February 1940):41–46, 53; and "Who and What is 'Negro?'" *Opportunity* 20 (March 1942), 83–87. These are reprinted in *The Critical Temper of Alain Locke*, 251–55, 291–97, 313–18.

79. Alain Locke and Bernhard J. Stern, eds. *When Peoples Meet: A Study in Race and Culture Contacts* (New York: Progressive Education Association, 1942).

80. E. Franklin Frazier, "Review of *When Peoples Meet: A Study in Race and Culture Contact*," *Science and Society* 6 (Winter 1942):93.

81. Alain Locke, "The Negro in the Three Americas," *Journal of Negro Education* 13 (Winter 1944):7–18.

82. Margaret Just Butcher, *The Negro in American Culture: Based on Materials left by Alain Locke* (New York: Alfred A. Knopf, 1956).

83. Locke, *American Philosophy Today and Tomorrow*, 313.

84. C. Vann Woodward, *The Origins of the New South* (Baton Rouge: Louisiana State University Press, 1951); *The Strange Career of Jim Crow* 3d ed. (London: Oxford University Press, 1974).

85. J. Morgan Kousser, *The Shaping of Southern Politics: Suffrage Restrictions and the Establishment of the One-Party South, 1880–1910* (New Haven: Yale University Press, 1974).

86. Oliver C. Cox, *Caste, Class and Race: A Study in Social Dynamics* (New York: Doubleday, 1948).

87. Edna Bonacich, "A Theory of Ethnic Antagonism: The Split Labor Market," *American Sociological Review* 37 (1972):547–59.

88. Winthrop D. Jordan, *White Over Black: American Attitudes Toward the Negro, 1550–1812* (Chapel Hill: University of North Carolina Press, 1968); David Brion Davis, *The Problem of Slavery in the Age of Revolution, 1770–1823* (Ithaca, N.Y.: Cornell University Press, 1975).

89. Steven Hahn, *The Roots of Southern Populism: Yeoman Farmers and the Transformation of the Georgia Upcountry, 1850–1890* (New York: Oxford University Pres, 1983), Jonathan M. Wiener, *Social Origins of the New South: Alabama, 1860–1885* (Baton Rouge: Louisiana University Press, 1978); Jay R. Mandle, *The Roots of Black Poverty: The Southern Plantation Economy After the Civil War* (Durham: Duke University Press, 1978).

90. Barbara Jeanne Fields, "Race and Ideology in American History" in J. Morgan Kousser and James MacPherson, eds. *Region, Race and Reconstruction: Essays in Honor of C. Vann Woodward* (New York: Oxford University Press, 1982), 143–77.

91. John W. Cell, *The Highest Stage of White Supremacy: The Origins in South Africa and the American South* (Cambridge: Cambridge University Press, 1985).

92. Ibid., 117.

93. John Rex, *Race Relations in Sociological Theory* (London: Weidenfeld & Nicolson, 1970).

94. Ibid., xi.

95. J. William Harris, "Etiquette, Lynching, and Boundaries: Racism as a Cultural System in Southern History," paper presented at the Research Seminar of the Program in Southern History at the University of California at San Diego, June 1989.

96. Houston A. Baker, Jr., *Blues, Ideology, and Afro-American Liteature: A Vernacular Theory* (Chicago: University of Chicago, 1984).

97. Richard Powell, et al., *The Blues Aesthetic: Black Culture and Modernism* (Washington: Washington Project for the Arts, 1989).

Editorial Practices

These lectures, originally titled, "Race Contacts and Inter-racial Relations: A Study of the Theory and Practice of Race," were first given in April and May of 1915; Locke delivered them again in March and April of 1916. Much later, as a visiting professor at Fisk University, he revised and delivered them in the spring semester of 1928. While Locke may have given these lectures at other times during his career, the only existing transcriptions in the Alain Locke Papers of the Moorland-Spingarn Research Center at Howard University in Washington, D.C. are of his presentations in 1916 and 1928. I have selected the 1916 transcriptions as the source text because they are the earliest and most complete version of these lectures: all five of the lectures in the 1916 version have survived, whereas only two of the 1928 lectures remain. The source text for "The Great Disillusionment," which is included in the appendix, is a hand-written original from the Alain Locke Papers.

My aim in editing these lectures is to retain as much fidelity to the transcriptions as possible. Thus, the original document has been presented as it exists, but with a number of emendations in brackets. The major problem with the transcriptions is their incompleteness: they were typed by a stenographer who missed, or omitted, many words, phrases, and sometimes sentences from Locke's lectures. With such large gaps in the transcriptions, some intervention by the editor has been necessary to make the lectures readable. Moreover, it is apparent that Locke wished to amend the documents: the 1916 transcriptions contain suggested words, phrases, and alterations in punctuation in Locke's handwriting in the body of the text and in the margins. Yet these corrections do not come close to rendering the entire text readable. In fairness to the author and the reader, some intervention by the editor is warranted to make the text readable. Where it has been necessary to change the text or delete words for readability, the changes and the deleted portions have been put in endnotes. While this procedure means a fair amount of notes in the text, I believe the distraction is outweighed by the reader having full knowledge of the changes I have made to the text.

My most important intervention has been to add missing words and phrases to fill in the gaps in the transcriptions, and to identify them as my own by placing them in roman letters and in brackets. In some cases, I consulted Locke's privately published *Syllabus to an Extension Course of Lectures on Race Contacts and Inter-Racial Relations* (1916) to obtain the sense of a passage. When it seemed that the syllabus supplied the exact phrase or sentence that was missing, I have borrowed it from the *Syllabus*, inserted it into the text where it fits, and indicated it with double angle brackets, ⟨⟨ ⟩⟩. Where Locke had written in missing words, or crossed out typed words and supplied his own written substitutions, I have included Locke's interpolations directly in the text, setting them off from the stenographer's words by placing Locke's in italics. In addition, someone else, probably the stenographer himself, has inserted words in the text and on the margins of the transcriptions. Where these words appear to supply a missing or better word, I have included them in the text and placed them in brackets and italics. Where there have been gaps, but the sentence made sense without interruption (perhaps suggesting that the gaps were the stenographer's pauses), I have silently continued the sentence without indicating the gaps. In a few cases, Locke has quoted from published sources, but the quotations have been incomplete or inaccurate. In those cases, I have consulted the published works, supplied the missing words or corrected incorrect words and indicated such insertions with double slashes, // //, and an endnote.

Other problems with the transcriptions exist as well. Even when a complete sentence was written down by the stenographer, some of the sentences remain confusing or even incomprehensible, because the word choice, word order, or syntax is wrong. Without attempting to improve the text, I have occasionally supplied an additional word or phrase in brackets when needed to clarify the meaning of a sentence. In the few cases in which the word supplied by the stenographer has been confusing, misleading, or disruptive of the syntax and another word has been clearer, I have supplied the needed word, placed it in brackets, and moved the original word to an endnote, where it can be consulted by the reader. Wherever a change in the word order or syntax of a sentence has been essential to clarify the meaning of a sentence or passage, I have changed the word order and placed the original version in an endnote. When a word has been changed or the word order altered, the note indicating that change in the text comes immediately before the change, except in those cases where the change occurs at the beginning of the sentence. In that case, the note follows the first word of the sentence.

In addition, the transcriptions contain numerous repetitious words and phrases, which detract from and sometimes obscure the meaning of a sentence. Where such repetitions have conveyed the rhythm of Locke's lecture style, I have retained them, but where superfluous words and short phrases have detracted from the clarity of a sentence, I have deleted them and placed them in a footnote. If a word or phrase has been deleted, the footnote occupies the space vacated. In a few cases, individual words have been circled, apparently by Locke, who, in proofreading the documents, may have discovered that inappropriate words had been introduced into the text. Where my own reading has confirmed that such words are inappropriate and were meant to be deleted, I have silently deleted them.

Locke was a notoriously poor speller; moreover, the stenographer appears not to have been familiar with many of the names of those persons to whom Locke referred; hence, there are many spelling mistakes in the transcriptions. For example, Locke habitually spelled the last name of the American anthropologist Franz Boas as "Boaz." I have silently corrected such errors; I also silently changed Locke's occasional English spelling and placement of punctuation into standard modern American usage. Both Locke and his stenographer appear to have had a penchant for idiosyncratic spelling, one of which was the habit of making two words out of one, as in the case of "promise-full": I have silently corrected these and deleted the unnecessary hyphens in such words. For the sake of grammar, I have made minor stylistic adjustments: for example, I have changed "concept" to "conception," where appropriate, replaced "in" with "into," where needed, and indicated these changes with brackets. I have also added or dropped the plural on verbs to ensure grammatical agreement with the subject of the sentence. The titles of books have been italicized.

The transcriptions contain idiosyncratic punctuation, being littered with dashes, where commas, parentheses, semicolons, or periods would normally be used. In most cases, this use of dashes is excessive even by 1916 standards. While the version presented here contains more dashes than usual in a document such as this, I have silently changed many dashes into commas, parentheses, semicolons, and periods to regularize the punctuation. Similarly, some sentences run on for several pages without punctuation of any kind. Where the absence of punctuation is not confusing, I have not added any. But when necessary for clarity, I have added commas or other punctuation, indicating that they are mine by placing them in brackets.

In general, I have retained the original paragraph breaks, and hence the manuscript as it appears here contains both more long paragraphs and one-sentence paragraphs than usual. To make the text more readable, however, I have occasionally introduced paragraph breaks or ignored those in the transcriptions and indicated the change in a footnote. Sometimes, very long sentences have been broken into shorter ones by adding a period (in brackets) and beginning the next sentence by capitalizing the first letter of the following word.

Individual lectures have posed special problems. The transcription of lecture 1, "The Theoretical and Scientific Conceptions of Race," was the most problematic. It had two first pages, one of which was torn, but contained Locke's handwritten emendations: I used that copy. The second page of the document was missing, which I indicated with a footnote. More generally, the first lecture, a review of anthropological research on race during Locke's time, was the most difficult to reconstruct. Not only were many words missing, but also even after words were supplied, the first lecture reads awkwardly, perhaps attesting to Locke's first-night jitters or to the complexity of the subject matter Locke was discussing.

The second lecture, "The Political and Practical Conceptions of Race," is much clearer and more focused, in part, perhaps, because Locke seems personally engaged in the discussion of the political uses of race under imperialism and missionarism—especially when discussing his experiences at the "Imperial Training School" Oxford. By contrast, the third lecture, "The Phenomena and Laws of Race Contacts," warms slowly to its argument after ten pages of Locke's justification of a scientific approach over the impressionistic analyses of more popular observers of race behavior. The reader's patience—as well as the editor's—is rewarded, however, for this lecture contains the heart of Locke's insights into the workings of race within a variety of social settings. As does the transcript of the first lecture, that of "The Phenomena and Laws of Race Contacts" contained many gaps. My reconstruction of this lecture relies more than the others on the published syllabus for clues to missing words and phrases. That syllabus also helped considerably in the reconstruction of lecture 4, "Modern Race Creeds and Their Fallacies." The transcription of the fifth and final lecture, "Racial Progress and Race Adjustment," required the least effort to edit. Not only did it have the fewest missing words, but it remains the clearest and the most straightforward presentation of the lectures.

The scholar who wishes to compare the original 1916 transcriptions of the lectures will find the surviving parts of the manuscript in the Alain Locke Papers at the Moorland-Spingarn Research Center at Howard University in Washington, D.C.

EDITORIAL SIGNS

[roman]	Encloses conjectural words or passages supplied by the editor.
italics	Indicates handwritten words or passages on the transcriptions supplied by Alain Locke.
[italics]	Indicates handwritten words or passages on the transcriptions supplied by someone other than Locke.
⟨⟨ ⟩⟩	Encloses excerpts inserted in the text from the pamphlet, *Race Contacts and Inter-Racial Relations: A Study in the Theory and Practice of Race: Syllabus of an Extension Course of Lectures* privately published by Locke.
// //	Encloses excerpts inserted in the text from quoted sources.

Race Contacts and Interracial Relations

1

The Theoretical
and Scientific Conceptions
of Race

L ADIES AND GENTLEMEN: Ever since the possibility of a comparative study of races dawned upon me at the Races Congress[1] in
London in 1911, I have had the courage of a very optimistic and
steadfast belief that in the scientific approach to the race question, there
was the possibility of a redemption for those false attitudes of mind
which have, unfortunately, so complicated the idea and conception of
race that there are a great many people who fancy that the best thing
that can possibly be done, *if possible at all*, is to throw *race* out of the
categories of human thinking.

At the same time, even if it were possible to eliminate the concept
that has been the center of so much social thinking, *let us not presume, at
least at the outset of a study professing a critical basis, that it would be desirable.*
I will grant you that the social thinking that has clustered about the
concept of race has been in *most* instances very paradoxical and in other
instances pernicious[.] And yet I cannot see how we can keep what is
good and wholly eliminate the evil unless it should be through a scientific scrutiny of the various meanings of race; to try, if possible, to
discriminate among them and to perpetuate, for better thinking in the
future, those meanings—those concepts—which are promising and
really sound.[2] I am fundamentally convinced that the term "race," the
thought of race, represents a rather fundamental category in social
thinking and that it is an idea that we can ill dispense with. In fact[,]the
more thought of the right kind [that] can be centered in it, the more

will the term [race] itself be redeemed, in the light of its rather unfortunate history. The only way to treat the subject scientifically is to regard it as a center of meaning. To[3] [develop a rational] concept of race [is] one of the unworked opportunities of social science, particularly because it is in the field of the social sciences that we must hope for a clarification of the idea and for the arrival at a final clear meaning.

What is race? That is the question which takes us back to the very root of the trouble. Race is not one thing—it is many things. In fact it has so many meanings that even were each meaning scientifically correct[,] there would necessarily arise conflict among such meanings, which would precipitate certain problems. When we reflect upon the possibility of this scientific confusion of meanings,[4] we see that in this problem of race we are confronting one of the most perplexing and one of the most [baffling] of problems that can confront the social thinker. And the extent to which we can clarify our concept determines the extent to which we can clarify our thinking [about][5] it. The only way in which the mind can influence practice is through this comprehending of the irrational meanings or clarifying rationalized meanings. The practice which is the reinforcement of reason must necessarily prevail. As reason begins to ferment within the meanings of an idea, we see a tendency towards clarification and a tendency towards the working out of some of the unfortunate foreign ferment, which has attended, really, the derivation of almost every useful concept that we know of in science. Race as such has undergone a history such as I have described.

Most of the fundamental concepts of the sciences [tend] to flounder through the vortex of just such a maelstrom of meanings[,] eventually to come out with one meaning superior to the others.

You can see that we are approaching this subject with, perhaps, something of the bias of a person interested in having the concept of race wrought out to a single clear meaning. Yet if it should be found impossible to arrive at such a meaning, then our goal would fall short of that and we would have to be content with simply discriminating the meanings so that they could not possibly be confused.

Abstract thinking about the terms of race is a matter of comparatively recent development. Most authorities agree that de Gobineau,[6] who wrote the *Essai sur l'inégalité des races humaines* in 1854, was the man who inaugurated [race theory as such.] Monsieur de Gobineau's attitude was that of an amateur in the social sciences and his whole aim seems to have been to draw a line of demarcation between what he called the "superior" and what he called the "inferior" races. The origin of most of that broad classification [of races] is not at all etymological, as you can see, but [has][7] so strangely insinuated itself into anthropological science. [But] anthropology is only supposed to be a descriptive science [and therefore] could establish no such standard as [a] *normative* standard between superior and inferior races.

Nevertheless, de Gobineau succeeded in developing[8] a classification of races, which[9] we shall have to deal with largely in this lecture. We should call that classification of races anthropological if it had not through anthropology spread through practically all descriptive science of *society*. It is therefore no less anthropological [nor] *ethnological* [than] it is[10] sociological. And the[11] *one vitiating* standard seems to have permeated the whole basis of descriptive social science. We do not claim that a great deal of this has not been scientific in method and in data. As a matter of fact, the race theory in the years since de Gobineau's work, I think, has been rather irreproachable as to scientific methods and scientific data. [And yet] we can all distinguish a science which is sane in method *from* a science which is sound in its conclusions. For that reason we can believe that[,] in spite of the accuracy of its methods, such science is largely pseudo-scientific both in its postulates and in its conclusions. It has set out, therefore, to prove something which has already been made a basic assumption of the science in question. It has devoted its[12] [research and methodology not toward a] descriptive end[, but toward proving the existence of] certain superior race types and certain inferior race types, and [toward showing] that the whole history of man confirms the original classification, an original classification which de Gobineau introduced into the science of race thought.

We should expect naturally that race theory should be a philosophy of the dominant groups. That is natural. That is inevitable. Further than that, we should expect that it would [make][13] some sort of brief for the prevailing types of civilization. But that[14] is the utmost concession we can make to a study of race that professes to be scientific[.] [And yet that] is far short of the end which really is aimed at by the current science of race[,] because the current science of race aimed really to go further. If [Gobineau and others like him][15] would frankly qualify this as the philosophy of a particular phase of civilization, or the justification of a particular type, then we could very well say that they had a certain admitted validity. But when they go further and claim that as an objective science there has been found or [established][16] anthropological and

3

ethnological evidence [of a hierarchy of race groups] among mankind [,and that civilization is the product solely of the higher race groups in this classification made] by de Gobineau[,] then we must admit that it has exceeded its limits, that it has gone further than[,] in any case[,] its scientific data have warranted[,] and that it is therefore based upon a fundamental contradiction, and upon an assumption which it is really beyond the province of any objective science to prove.

The anthropological and ethnological evidence which has been adduced in favor of the modern theories is quite enormous, too enormous, in fact, for us to go into in any considerable detail[.] And yet[,] if we should neglect to examine[17] it at least to the degree of proving that it is based upon a fallacy, we should have neglected the first opportunity that presents itself for clarifying the conception of race. If these theories remained on the [level][18] of descriptive science, it would make very little difference how many classifications were made. It would make very little difference because the designations would be merely categories or descriptions [of race types. We would have little argument with the] prevailing terms of race if they were used [merely] as descriptive categories[.] But when carried further and made the basis for normative principles of mankind, they become the most iniquitous of the scientific conclusions of an age which, say what you will, has at least given us as much false science as it has of true science.

This first generation of race theorists [has][19] at least come to the conclusion that the warrant of the scientific method is at stake and that unless they retract at least some of the extreme assertions that have been made, their whole social science stands in danger of being undermined and controverted.[20] Consequently[,] there has been an extraordinary reaction in purely scientific circles for purely scientific reasons.[21] Most particularly, the French and the German anthropologists have protested against any carrying of the descriptive classifications into classes [of humanity,] into concepts of race [superiority and inferiority.] Through the anthropological and the ethnological [research they have produced, they] have tried to illustrate [the limitations of anthropological observations] in order to protect their scientific method. The earliest of these [were] those German anthropologists, of whom [Johann] Blumen[bach][22] is really the most to be admired. Finot,[23] coming considerably later, a man of perhaps unchallenged authority in the field of the anthropological sciences, feels that it is the broad aim of anthropological science today to have the false categories (or at least the false use of the categories) of race swept out of these social sciences. Consequently[,] he has, in a very painstaking way (almost too painstaking a way, I fancy) tried to demolish what are, after all, the *idols* of the [older] anthropologists. [These modern anthropologists have advanced] the idea that the physical differences of men (those anthropological differences which are most useful in anthropology)[24] have no meaning other than for purposes of descriptive classification[.] [They substantiate this claim by] proving that these anthropological factors are in themselves both subject to change and perfectly unreliable as clues to any sociological meaning of the term "race[.]" Because it is manifest that if these factors, instead of being static, are variable—that they simply register the biological history of the particular group—[then there is no stable physical basis for the sociological concept of race.] And since that biological history is in itself on such a scale as to be incommensurate with the social history of the same group, and that there is, of course, no parallel between the anthropological factors of a race and its position in social culture or adaptability for social culture, [any judgment about the influence of biological factors on social culture] is a false and a very risky deduction. More than that, there still prevails, in spite of the almost colossal amount of evidence that has been inveighed against it, the idea that after all there is some special virtue in classifying mankind in terms of anthropological factors, instead of using the anthropological factors as clues to various environmental influences which all groups have at some time had to pass through, and of which there is at least anthropological record within every race group that you can possibly think of.

Because of differences [in][25] anthropological [factors,] anthropological points of comparison have now been reduced to such a narrow margin in each instance that the variations between individuals of the same race, and even the same nation, more than outspan the maximum variability between what are regarded[26] as cognate races of mankind. To put it in terms of a concrete example, one can find more variability in the [anthropological differences] between one class of Frenchmen and another class of Frenchmen than when you take an average European and [compare him with] an [average] African or a Malay. We may find between men of different historical periods of the same country a considerably wider variation than between, for example, the men of prehistoric ages or the men who evidently seem to be descended from them ethnologically.

5

So the point in the [modern view is that, because there is so considerable a degree of] variation [within a race group, many] anthropological
differences [between the races] are lost.[27] And [the older view of the
racial significance of anthropological differences] must give place, if anthropological science is to progress, to simply the description of anthropological factors as clues to the environmental and biological influences
which have been at work during long periods of history upon this or
that group of people. Now, of course, in some quarters this discrediting
of the older anthropology has led to a reaction against anthropological
data altogether, which is rather unfortunate, because no one could
possibly refuse to recognize the importance of anthropology and of
ethnology. It has not been the data, but the use of the data that has
been reprehensible and that must be corrected[;] and it would be rather
unfortunate should the next generation of scholars repudiate, upon the
basis of these facts, these sciences which are yet in their infancy.

Nevertheless, as the outcome of it, there has been, even among the
anthropologists themselves, a tendency toward [recognition of] another
kind of factor[, the sociological factor]. The sociological factors have
been the factors which have appealed and which are appealing to the
more enlightened of the present day generation of scholars or students
of human society.

We might say[28] in passing, that it is extraordinarily strange that just at
the time when evolution was dominant in the scientific world, that to
anthropology and ethnology, almost all of the factors were not evolutionary factors at all. [According to these first generation race theorists,]
there is not an anthropological factor which even shows a hint of becoming dynamic. All are static. All are regarded as if they were not
variable, when the whole weight of evidence shows them as merely the
results of environmental adaptation, which, of course, is the variable
factor in evolutionary science. For that reason there has been a double
reaction. In the first place, [there has been an increased regard for
investigating the role of] sociological data [in shaping human development,] and in the second place, [there has been increased acknowledgment of the] [dynamic][29] [character] of these data of race.

There came upon the scene very shortly after this [first generation of
race theorists] another school of social science[, whose thinkers][30] have
been believers in social psychology and have said that the only possible
factors that could be of real use were those that should reveal group
traits, but traits that are mental. [These are] traits that actually differen-

tiated not only mental capacity but mental reactions. This school of the social psychologists would have us believe that the entire solution of the science of race lies within the borders of this rather newly discovered aspect of psychology.

There is no doubt that there remains to be developed an [analysis of the] enormous amount of facts discovered by the social psychologists which[,] when brought to bear upon the anthropological factors which have previously been brought forward[,] will doubtless reveal some very significant differences [and] some very significant similarities, I imagine, among men. But it is false to think that ethno-psychology, as it is called, will exhaust the almost [limitless] question of "What is race?" Within the narrow limits of that science, no more definite answer could possibly be arrived at than has already been arrived at in the sciences, in the development of which, [we have seen important new changes occur in] their attitude toward the designation of race.

Since it is a social science,[31] race theory—our course—is something that has and must have correlation with our practical ideas of human society. It must reinforce what is currently believed about human society. It may sometimes go in advance of that, but always there will be the pull of what men currently think human society is and, I fancy[,] we shall be very well advised and not so apt to be disillusioned if we frankly claim and admit that race theory is essentially committed to the historical bias.

It is something which, like history itself, must incorporate the factor of human belief, because history is not merely a record of facts but, as well, a record of beliefs, and an historical opinion (be it an individual opinion or a group opinion) [which] is as important a factor of history as the objective fact itself. Therefore[,] what men think race to be depends in a large measure upon what they practically think human society to be. And with every changed concept[ion] of human society, undoubtedly a chang[ed] emphasis upon this or on that aspect of the concept of race will follow, just as inevitably as such emphasis follows in history itself.

Meanwhile, what of a pure science of race? Is it necessary? Is it desirable? Is it possible if it were desirable and necessary? I fancy that in the present state of the sciences of [man,] it must be admitted impossible. That seems to be the frank conclusion of the most recent scholars in this field, particularly Professor [Franz] Boas[32] in America and Dr. [Friedrich] Hertz[33] and Dr. [Felix] von Luschan[34] in Germany, [all of whom] have come to this conclusion after a very long attempt to pursue the subject upon a very rigid scientific basis. They believe that a really pure science of race is, after all, undesirable, not so much because it is impossible, but because even though it were realized, it would be impracticable, particularly as contrasted with whatever current practical theories of race are prevailing in society. It could never sucessfully hope to compete with what men really believe human society to be. Consequently[,] they seem perfectly reconciled to a more or less modified scientific conception of race[,] rather than attempt to take the actual practical conceptions that constitute society to be thus upon a scientific basis. It is the idea[,] then[,] that instead of a perfectly objective science of human society, that we should have a corrective or a normative conception of society which should aim to improve upon and better those predominant notions and ideals which are prevalent.

After all, we have very little use for a merely abstract science of race. It only comes into requisition when we are concerned over [groups in widely divergent] historical periods and in [the] contrast between extremely divergent groups [such] as between absolute savages and modern men, or as between the modern man and a prehistoric man[.][35] It is upon this level that modern anthropology and ethnology have been really successful, or rather it is upon this level that they have achieved what must be regarded as their permanent results. We are not [likely to have a][36] purely objective science of race.

One would not think of challenging the scientific accuracy of the contemporary practices of both ethnology and anthropology. Until, however, there shall come some scientific correlation between biological and sociological [factors,] we must realize that there is a limit placed upon the science of race[.] It[37] is only [useful] from the scientific point of view [when] dealing with social origins [of] primitive groups and practices, as a guide to the relative value of the hereditary and the environmental influences upon social groups. There is its field, and within that jurisdiction it undoubtedly has enough unsolved problems to keep it busy a half-century or more; and the tendency among recent scientists is to accept that and not to go out of it, feeling that until these problems have been satisfactorily solved, any application of the strictly scientific criteria and factors to their problems in human society is perfectly irrelevant[.] [They make that judgment] upon the principle that until one's own house is put in order, one is really not in a position at all to interfere even with the untidy housekeeping of others.

The [modern scientific] tendency, then, is in the nature of a reaction to the strictly limited, and the strictly necessary field in which anthropology and ethnology must grope[.][38] [Modern researchers are seeking to formulate] some scientific conceptions of the early phases and stages of social culture of the primitive types, and of the order in which these primitive types have [evolved, and of] the effect of environment and heredity upon the social system in [sorting humanity] into the [race] types which at the present time prevail.

These types which we find at present are undoubtedly the [focus of attention] in anthropological science.[39] We have them here and our business is to explain them. It seems rather to have been the business of the early phases of the science we are criticizing, not to have explained them, but to justify them, which is, of course, quite another thing. No one can tell how much they are going to change, or at what rate[.] They are observed, [however,] to [exist][40] at present.[41] Other sciences thus show themselves as yet unable even to interpret how they came about. Consequently, limiting itself to the explanation of racial differences as they are, anthropological science finds itself still confronted with its proper problem.

Racial differences parallel what we know in human society as racial inequalities.[42] Now, what do we mean by that? It is an unfortunate parallel, but it is a fact. But it is not necessary to argue that racial differences and racial inequalities are cause and effect, for they may not be. Yet it is true that historical[,] economic[,] and social causes have led to certain differentiations in social culture and in civilization types which unfortunately coincide with these racial differences of the physiological and anthropological sort, which are the particular concern of the phases of science which we have just discussed. And yet, in spite of this parallelism, there is in the more narrow [view, an assumption that racial inequalities are caused by racial differences,] and if we will only rid ourselves of that assumption which comes really from our instincts rather than from science itself, we shall, I fancy, be far on the way to seeing a clear goal ahead of us. [Science will eventually prove what is already suggested by the best contemporary research[,] that is[,] that we should] differentiat[e][43] between racial differences and race inequalities, explaining the race inequalities in terms of historical, economic, and social factors, and explaining the racial differences in terms of anthropological and ethnological factors[,] and predicating another cause and effect [basis for the] relation between the two.

The reason that causes us to believe that science will ultimately arrive at such a position is the fact that there are no static factors of race at all.[44] Even the anthropological factors are variable, and pseudo-scientific except for purposes of descriptive classification. The factors which really determine race inequalities (that is to say inequalities and differences of social culture as between one ethnic group, or one ethnic unit, and another) are factors which are not at all commensurable with these physical factors. They are factors of language, customs, habits, social adaptability, [and] social survival—historical factors of what may have been the actual fate of groups of people. Because within every ethnic group there are prevalent such inequalities determined by traceable historical conditions[,] in which we find one branch of people prospering in social culture, and another branch of the same group not prospering.

This is perhaps nowhere better illustrated than in the case of the social culture of the two branches of the Semitic peoples—the so-called German Jew and the [*Abyssinian*] Jew. There exists between these two wings of the same ethnic group [an] identity more strictly in history than any [other ethnic group] we know of. [And yet] there is between these two[,] more difference in social culture and in capacity for social culture than the differences noted between the so-called "inferior" races and the so-called "superior" races. Therefore[,] it is evident that race inequalities must have an historical explanation, and that they should be traced to historical causes and regarded as factors of a people's history. So that we see people going through history with the birthmark of history upon them. We see them going through with the scars and the traces of almost every contact and influence to which they have been subject[.] And we find that what we know as race prejudice is really fundamentally based upon the differences in social culture and the differences in type of civilization. But we have [a] difference which is a difference in the social consciousness of groups, strangely enough assigned and baselessly assigned to the very biological and anthropological factors which we have shown have no connection with them[,] excepting an accidental one. Therefore[,] race prejudice is so paradoxical a thing that we must define it as an almost instinctive aberration in favor of anthropological factors erected into social distinctions—there being, of course, no commensurability between the one type of factor and the other.

If we are going to redeem [this] suggestion which prevails, unfortunately, just as much in our science as in our popular thinking, we shall have to have an appropriate set of factors in terms of which to express race inequalities. Race inequalities need to be correlated and defined, and they need to be explained,[45] and honorably explained, even, in fact, those [inequalities] which happen to be unfortunate. If only some evolutionary and dynamic factors can be found which shall express, not the descriptive classifications and distinctions of anthropological science, but differences in civilization types and differences in culture stages, then we shall be upon the verge of the realization of a real science of human society which can account for the superiorities—the real, the admitted, and the unchallenged superiorities at certain periods, of certain ethnic groups and certain civilization types. The distinctions which are directly involved in anthropological descriptive science are so justifiable and necessary in the other sciences of human society that not to know what are primary and what [are]secondary[,] what [are] relatively higher, and what are relatively lower states of culture [handicaps other scientific research on society.] We need to know what is better [and] perhaps what is the best [of] civilized types.[46]

Consequently, any true history of race must be a sociological theory of race.[47] [It] must be a theory of culture stages and of social evolution[,] and must interpret in terms of one and the same principle[, the accomplishments of all ethnic groups and civilizations,] so that the superiorities and the inferiorities, or let us say to be really more scientific, [the] successes and the failures of one ethnic group or another ethnic group, one type of civilization as contrasted with another type of civilization, one stage of civilization as contrasted with another stage of civilization[, will be explained consistently.]

Really, when the modern man talks about race[,] he is not talking about the anthropological or biological idea at all. [He is really talking about the historical record of success or failure of] an ethnic group. As I pointed out, these groups, from the point of view of anthropology, are ethnic fictions. This does not mean that they do not exist[,] but it can be shown [that these groups do] not[48] have as [permanent] designations those very factors upon which they pride themselves. They have neither purity of [blood] nor purity of type. They are the products of countless interminglings of types[,] and they are the results of infinite crossings of types[.][49] They, however, maintain in name only this fetish of biological [purity.] Race as applied to social and ethnic groups has no meaning at all beyond that sense of kind, that sense of kith and kin which undoubtedly is somewhat of an advantage to any ethnic group that can maintain

[it]. And yet, useful as it is, it is not to deny its usefulness that we call it an ethnic fiction.

The[50] biological meaning of race has lapsed and the sociological meaning of race is growing in significance. While it may be that the social perpetuation of race is legitimate and necessary in the interest of the development of civilization, we must further admit that it is of advantage to a group when it can consider itself an ethnic unit[.] But that the group needs to consider itself an ethnic unit is very different from the view that the group is an ethnic unit. That the stimulus of race sense is an additional incentive to civilization is no proof that civilization has developed merely according to the inherent racial stimulus and [not been][51] projected onto the group really by their external objective fortunes.

Race is[,] at present then, in a paradoxical stage. It amounts practically to social inheritance[,] and yet it parades itself as biological or anthropological inheritance. It really is either favorable or unfavorable social inheritance, which has been ascribed to anthropological differences. To the extent, therefore, that any man has race, he has inherited either a favorable or an unfavorable social heredity, which unfortunately is [typically] ascribed to factors which have not produced [it,] factors which will in no way determine either the period of those inequalities or their eradication. They must be perpetuated along different lines in so far as they are permanent[,] and they must be eradicated, generally, along different lines in so far as they are [transitory.] And although there is a certain factor of permanence in them, the encouraging thing is that from the minutest biological factor to the subtlest social factor, there can be discovered no factor at present which is static—which is not subject to chance and variation. What is subject to change and variation is at least subject to either degeneration or improvement[;] and it simply is [a question of] history and human [will] as to which direction, positive or negative, that curve shall take.

Where there is any variable factor, there is possibility of change. There is possibility of change forward or backward, in one direction or the other[.] We have, however, [to] regard the science of race as having at least proven to us that race is something which[,] from the social sense[,] is capable of development, and something which[,] from the biological sense[,] is certainly capable of practical [reorientation] in terms of the social factors which, after all, are the more meaningful[,] and the more significant of the factors that can be discriminated. Therefore, race prejudice as it exists today is something which has simply the status of a social paradox, something which, in spite of its prevalence and in spite of its appeal to almost ineradicable human instincts, is something that can be confuted by science[,] and that in time may, with the aid of [science, gain] the negative advantage of this answer [to the question, are racial characteristics biologically determined?] This answer, which, after all is the answer that the modern theories of race do give [is that] race as social inheritance is not race as biological inheritance, and though they have the one goal, they are in no way so interdependent that one can argue from one to the other[.] And[52] although, undoubtedly, there is in the practical world[,] as in the scientific world, some necessary classification of mankind according to these anthropological factors, the ultimate classification of men in[to] the civilization types and groups[,] and [into] their roles in the advancement of civilization[53] to this or that particular stage of social culture[, is traceable to social and historical factors]. There can be[,] with respect to these, no ultimate handicap from the biological factors which may[,] for descriptive purposes[,]remain permanent[.] Because the social classification will change with changes of social condition, and it may very well be that[,] in the social concept of race[,] there is that ultimate contradiction of the biological concept of race, except from the point of view [of the older, pseudo-scientific race theorists. It may well be that acceptance of the sociological concept of race will bring about] that descriptive biological science that really seems to us[54] [to be fair and desirable, and for which we] so devoutly wish—particularly those of us that are the victims of the [negative] social type of inheritance.

And yet, wishing this, we should not be guilty of the same fallacy that I described at the beginning of this lecture. We should not predicate our postulates[, and] we should not forge our hopes and wishes into social views or into social theories. Social views and social theories must be investigated and must be given their answer upon a scientific basis. Though we need to study the question of race still further[, we] hop[e][55] to have clarified this time, perhaps, some of the fundamental conceptions of race, which[,] undoubtedly[,] come to us in theory from the anthropological science of the last century.

With the present state of world civilization, views as a whole [are tending toward a new view of the role of race contacts] in human history. It is a [realization of the inevitability] of a world civilization which has never before been practically attained. There is no part of the universe today which is not in some way, economic[,] or political[,] or social, bound up with the other parts[;] and further[,] there is no possible [alternative] on this basis to a world contact and a world civilization. By "world civilization" we do not necessarily mean an approximation to a single type of social culture, but we do mean that no social culture in the present day world will be ignorant of other types or object to [some kind of] contact with other types, which certainly means that no matter how much a line is drawn theoretically between races, the practical demands of present day life necessitate the contact of races, and an increasing contact of races[.] And if so, it would seem that the very nature of modern civilization itself [demands] a regeneration of the false conceptions of race which have aimed at least to thwart [racial progress] or to turn to unfavorable tendencies the contacts between races of divergent [social culture] and divergent heredity.

False conceptions of race[,] therefore[,] are an obstacle to modern progress and a menace to modern civilization[, and they] need to be exterminated if possible by the cooperation of as many scientific [investigations] as is possible. And we shall hope in the succeeding lectures to turn our attention to some of these [other false conceptions of race] which are as significant and, it seems to me, as difficult as the one I have pointed out to you this evening.

N.B. In these notes, the symbols used to indicate gaps in the original transcriptions are as follows: [...] for gaps of one to three words, [....] for gaps of four to seven words, and [.....] for gaps of seven words or more. In the textural notes, punctuation is placed outside of the quotation marks that surround the original material to insure that the reader knows precisely what has been omitted or replaced. Unless otherwise noted, all correspondence cited is in the Alain Locke Papers at the Moorland-Spingarn Research Center at Howard University, referred to as ALP, HU.

NOTES: LECTURE 1

1. The First Universal Races Congress was held 26–29 July 1911 at the University of London, England. Dr. Felix Adler, the founder of the Ethical Culture Society, and Gustav Spiller, the man behind the London Ethical Culture movement, called this conference to promote greater understanding between the East and the West. More than fifty social scientists, statesmen, and speakers from around the world were invited to share the latest theoretical and practical information on race and race relations in Asia, Europe, the Middle East, and the United States. Professors Franz Boas, Alfred Fouillee, Charles S. Myers, and Earl Finch discussed the latest findings in the study of the relation of physical racial types (and/or heredity) on physical, social, and intellectual development of peoples. Other papers by Israel Zangwill, W. E. B. Du Bois, and General Legitime focused on the

practical problems of racial progress in the twentieth century. Locke's name did not appear on the list of visitors, but Locke traveled to London early in July of 1911, ostensibly to attend the conference. Given his use of information from that conference in his 1916 lectures, Locke probably attended the conference. See G. Spiller, ed. *Inter-Racial Problems: Papers from the First Universal Races Congress Held in London in 1911*, with a new introduction by Herbert Aptheker (New York: Citadel Press, 1970; orig. pub. 1911), [1] of introduction; and correspondence between De Fonseka to Alain Locke, 2 July 1911, 2 September 1911, and Mary Locke to Alain Locke, 24 July 1911, ALP, HU.

2. Words deleted following "really sound": "which are".

3. "To" is the last word on page 1 of the transcription; page 2 of the transcription is missing from the copy in ALP, HU. I have continued onto page 3 without interruption.

4. Words deleted following "meanings,": "in special groups".

5. "about" replaces original "of".

6. Joseph Arthur Comte de Gobineau (1816–82) was a French nobleman, a career diplomat, and a prolific writer on a variety of subjects. Born at Ville d'Avray outside Paris, Gobineau attended school at the College of Bienne in Switzerland. For a time he served as secretary to Alexis de Tocqueville, before becoming a diplomat, first to Persia in 1854, then to Greece, Brazil, and Sweden, where he ended his diplomatic career in 1876. Gobineau authored numerous books, including several respected novels, but he is best known as the author of *Essai sur l'inégalité des races humaines*, which was published in four volumes from 1853 to 1855. Gobineau was the first to make racial inequality and racial intermixture the key to the rise and fall of civilization. He ranked racial groups according to their capacities to originate independently civilization, and he believed such capacities were innate, and unaffected by changes in climatic or institutional environment. Civilizations declined when the Aryan, or "civilizing" stock of the white race, was diluted by too much intermixture with inferior races. Racial intermixture was not always bad; although contact with the inferior Semitic and African races had destroyed the Roman Empire, Rome's subsequent invasion by conquering Teutonic tribes had saved Western civilization. Gobineau believed that blacks were the lowest race of all, and provided in *Essai* a scathing, burlesque description of Haiti to prove that blacks could never independently achieve civilization. As an aristocrat, Gobineau favored fixed social orders, such as the Indian caste system over the more fluid system of classes and values produced by modern industrial capitalism. Accordingly, Gobineau believed that modern Europe faced certain degeneration, since the Aryan tendency to conquer actually increased contact—and intermixture—with the yellow and black races. In his day, Gobineau was credited with inaugurating the "scientific" treatment of civilization in terms of race, perhaps because he purported to reveal through his analysis of race, the hidden, motive force in history. But the pretentions to a "science of race" derived more from his supporters and followers, most notably the Germans, Richard Wagner and, subsequently, Wagner's naturalized son-in-law, Houston Stewart Chamberlain, who helped disseminate Gobineau's views as confirmation of German national superiority. Also enthusiastic was Mobile, Alabama physician Josiah Nott, who, despite Gobineau's rejection of Nott's theory of the multiple origins of mankind, helped publish part of the *Essai* in the United States in 1856 under the title, *The Moral and Intellectual Diversity of Races*. (Gobineau, *The Inequality of the Races*, translated by Adrian Collins (New York: H. Fertig, 1967; orig. pub. 1915), 48–49, *passim*; *Dictionnaire de Biographies* (Paris: Presses Universitaires de France, 1958), 613; *The McGraw-Hill Encyclopedia of World Biography* (New York: McGraw Hill, 1973), 429–30.)

7. "has" replaces original "which"; word order changed. Original: "strangely so insinuated".

8. Words deleted following "developing": "in favor of".

9. Words deleted following "which": "a classification of races".

10. Words deleted following "is": "no less".
11. Words deleted following "the": "only and the only".
12. Word deleted following "its": "or".
13. "make" replaces original "hold".
14. Word deleted following "that": "which".
15. "Gobineau and others like him" replaces original "they".
16. "established" replaces original "framed up".
17. Word deleted following "examine": "into".
18. "level" replaces original "basis".
19. "has" replaces original "have".
20. Paragraph break inserted at beginning of the sentence.
21. Irretrievable sentence deleted following "reasons.": "From the first generation [...] this race theory, which was instituted in the middle of the last century."

22. Locke gives "Blumenthol" in the original but most likely means Johann Friedrich Blumenbach (1752–1840), the University of Gottingen professor of medicine, who was one of the founders of anthropology. In his doctoral thesis, *On the Natural Variety of Mankind* (1775), Blumenbach argued for the unity of mankind, and suggested that the different races were simply the five varieties—Caucasian, Ethiopian, Mongolian, American, and Malay—into which a single human species was divided. He did believe in a hierarchy of race groups, with the Caucasian—a word he coined—being the primary race group and the most beautiful. But Blumenbach, like other race theorists of the Enlightenment, argued that such perceived differences were the product of environmental conditions, and thus were not permanent. When discussing the "Ethiopian variety" in *On the Natural Variety of Mankind*, he discounted claims that black people constituted a separate species because of their difference from Caucasians in color, or because of their presumed facial resemblance to apes, by noting that "there is no single character so peculiar and so universal among the Ethiopians, but what it may be observed on the one hand everywhere in other varieties of men." *(The Anthropological Treatises of Johann Friedrich Blumenbach, With Memoirs of Him By Marx and Flourens, and an Account of his Anthropological Museum by Professor R. Wagner, and the Inaugural Dissertation of John Hunter, M.D. on the Varieties of Man*, translated and edited by Thomas Bendyshe (Boston: Milford House, 1973; orig. pub. 1865), 270. (Thomas F. Gossett, *Race: The History of an Idea in America* (Dallas: Southern Methodist University Press, 1963), 37–39, 70, 80.)

23. Jean Finckelhaus Finot (1858–1922) was a naturalized French citizen, who was born in Warsaw and attended the University of Cambridge as well as the Faculty of Letters in Paris. He edited a number of magazines, most important the *Revue des Revues* which, under his direction after 1890, published some of the most provocative social, political, and philosophical studies appearing in the French press of his day. Finot is most known for his own monographs, including *La philosophie de la longévité* (1900), *Préjugé et probleme des sexes* (1913), and *Le préjugé des races* (1905), which was translated by Florence Wade-Evans and published by Dutton and Co. as *Race Prejudice* in 1907. *Race Prejudice* rebuts the notion that science justifies a belief in racial inequality. Finot uses anthropological and archaeological evidence to challenge the reliability of contemporary divisions of mankind, the craniological bases offered for such divisions, and the idea of color as the key to race integrity. Finot is especially critical of the notion that any physical or mental characteristic is permanent and concludes that *milieu* is the dominant factor in human evolution, not heredity. He also concludes that it is impossible to judge accurately the racial composition of a people, and, therefore, that it remains absurd to argue, as Gobineau and others have, that the success of a nation is due to the presence of a certain racial stock. *(Race Prejudice* (1907), xi, 40–75, 97, 150; *Dictionnaire de Biographie Française*, vol. 13 (Paris: Librairie Letouzey et Ane, 1975), 1376–77.)

24. Words deleted following "anthropology": "but which".

25. "in" replaces original "of".

26. Word deleted following "regarded": "by".

27. Paragraph break at beginning of the sentence.

28. Word order changed. Original: "We might say [...] that it is extraordinarily strange in passing, that just...."

29. "dynamic" replaces original "dynamical".

30. "whose thinkers" replaces original sentence fragments "[...] that it would lead us to believe that the differences of race must [....] so far as scientific solution is concerned, upon the level of anthropology and ethnology. They".

31. Word order changed. Original: "Race theory—our course—since it is a social science...."

32. Dr. Franz Boas (1858–1942) was the father of American anthropology and the most important critic of racial theories that asserted the permanency of racial characteristics. Born in Minden, Germany, Boas studied at Heidelberg, Bonn, and at the University at Kiel, where he earned his doctor of philosophy degree in physics. He had also studied geography, and while on a field trip to the Arctic, developed an interest in Eskimo culture, which later led him into the field of anthropology. He moved to the United States in 1887, and held positions at Clark University, the Field Museum in Chicago, and at the American Museum of Natural History—the last position held while also a professor of anthropology at Columbia University. There he trained such famous graduate students as Ruth Benedict and Melville Herskovits who went on to shape American anthropology profoundly. Boas was responsible for many innovations in modern anthropology. He was the first modern anthropologist to speak of cultures rather than Culture, to argue that so-called primitive societies had cultures which were as complex as those of modern man, and to suggest that civilization was actually the product of interchange between groups, rather than the exclusive offspring of one race, as Gobineau had suggested. In terms of race theory, Boas's most important contribution appeared in his essay, "The Instability of Human Types," delivered at the First Universal Races Congress, and later published as part of his pioneer work, *The Mind of Primitive Man* (1911). This essay reported Boas's findings from research conducted under the auspices of the Dillingham Commission on Immigration of the U. S. Congress, in which Boas tested the head size of immigrants to determine the role of environment in human physical traits. Boas found that Europeans underwent certain changes as a result of their living in the American environment, specifically that the head size of European-born individuals changed almost immediately after coming to the United States. Boas concluded that if the physical form of humans could change because of environment, then mental or cultural traits could also change, thus contradicting the main assertion of the Gobineau school that environment had little or no effect on the physical and mental characteristics of a race, and weakening the argument that heredity was the major factor determining racial character. Boas was perhaps the most important speaker Locke heard at the First Universal Races Congress, for Boas was conducting the kind of research that others at the Congress cited in their papers. See Brajendranath Seal's "Meaning of Race, Tribe, Nation," in Spiller's *Inter-Racial Problems*, 1–3. Boas's "Instability of Human Types" appears in Spiller's *Inter-Racial Problems*, 99–108; see "Foreword" by Melville Herskovits in *The Mind of Primitive Man*, rev. ed. (New York: Collier Books, 1963; orig. pub. 1911), 5–12.

33. Friedrich Otto Hertz (1878–1964) was born in Vienna, where he attended high school and university before attending the University of Munich and the University of London. He was secretary of the main union of Austrian industry, and in 1930–33, he was

professor of political economy and sociology at the University of Halle. His three areas of research were political economy, sociology, and social history. He published several books on race and nationalism, *Moderne Rassentheorien* (Vienna: C.W. Stern, 1904), which Locke cited in the pamphlet; *Rasse und Kultur*, (Leipzig: A. Kroner, 1925); and *Nationalgeist und Politik* (Zurich: Europa-verlag, 1937) after Hertz had migrated to England in the 1930s. In *Rasse und Kultur*, an updated version of *Moderne Rassentheorien*, Hertz provided an extended critique of the notion, propounded by Gobineau and Houston Stewart Chamberlain, that only the Aryan race was responsible for creating civilization. Moreover, Hertz argued that there was no physical basis for mental traits, that race mixing did not cause the decline of the Roman Empire, and that race did not limit the ability of a group to assimilate the cultural heritage of another race. (*Race and Civilization*, translated into English by A. S. Levetus and W. Entz (New York: Ktav Pub. House, 1970; orig. pub. 1928) 48–59, 137–47, 245–66; *Neue Deutsche Biographie* (Berlin: Duncker & Humblot, 1968) 709–10.)

34. Dr. Felix von Luschan was professor of anthropology at the University of Berlin and delivered the paper entitled, "Anthropological View of Race" at the First Universal Races Congress in 1911. In his congress speech he says that "serious scientists have tried in vain to draw up an exact definition of what really constitutes the difference between savage and civilised races." See Spiller's *Inter-Racial Problems*, 14. Von Luschan undermines the traditional bases for race superiority, arguing that color is a product of environment, that many dark skinned peoples have a highly developed religion and civilized life style, that Africans are among the cleanest people, and that the belief in mental inferiority of savages comes mainly from the awkward, stupid, and violent treatment of subjects interviewed by the Europeans themselves. Von Luschan, however, ends his speech upholding racial separation as uneradicable for the time being, and also gets in some saber rattling against England! See Aptheker's introduction in Spiller's *Inter-Racial Problems*, 4.

35. Located here in the original, the sentence "We are not having purely objective science of race and" was moved to end of paragraph.

36. "likely to have" replaces original "having".

37. Words deleted from beginning of sentence: "and that".

38. Word deleted following "grope": "for".

39. Paragraph break inserted at beginning of sentence.

40. "exist" replaces original "be".

41. Irretrievable sentence fragment deleted following "present.": "Consequently a [....] is something which is permanent, something the future course of which can be predicated and is simply translation [....]".

42. Paragraph break inserted at beginning of sentence.

43. "differentiate" replaces original "in differentiating".

44. Paragraph break inserted at beginning of sentence.

45. Word order changed. Original: "they need to be explained—explained [...] and honorably...."

46. Irretrievable sentence fragment deleted following "types.": "We know that in terms of factors which have [...] and from these differences which factors are variable [...] will be factors of the type that I have pointed out."

47. Paragraph break inserted at beginning of sentence.

48. Word deleted following "not": "to".

49. Word deleted following "types": "And".

50. Irretrievable sentence deleted at beginning of paragraph "This is something [...] science should know [...] and possess [...] therefore that true basis of race is to [....] and we must say that...."

51. "not been" replaces original "...and [...] that is".

52. Word order changed. Original: "and that although there is undoubtedly".

53. Words deleted following "civilization": "as readily".

54. Word order changed. Original: "to us [...]—particularly those of us that are the victims of the social type of inheritance, so devoutly wish."

55. Word order changed. Original: "[...] hoping this time perhaps to have clarified".

2

The Political and Practical Conceptions of Race

I N THE FIRST lecture we attempted to follow some of the modern
theories of race. These theories and an understanding of them are
necessary, really, for the considerations which we now undertake.[1]
[T]he considerations[2] we now undertake antedate, by centuries, those
that we have been considering[,] because the practices of race are world-
old, and[3] only the theory is modern. The world very often begins to
practice a thing long before it begins to speculate about it, and[4] the
world has been at work in terms of race long before it has ever come to
anything like a conception of race in the scientific sense.

The sense of race really almost antedates anything in its name, in the
etymology of it, because just as long as you have groups of people knit
together by a kinship feeling and [who] realiz[e] that[5] different practices
[operate in][6] their society from those which [operate in other societies
and therefore][7] determine their treatment of other groups, [then] you
really have what is the germ [of] the race sense.

The race sense, as you see, is something which is not vicious in itself,
but which may become so if invidious social practices are based upon it.
Consequently, we must trace the history of the practices of race from
these rather unseen beginnings in the group sense of various peoples,
for it is in this that the real distinctions of race, the practical distinctions,
originate. [We find the earliest race sense] [w]here people feel that there
is something in kinship relationship which makes a great difference and
makes one code prevail among them and another code prevail among

their neighbors—or those who really in a sense are not yet their neighbors, because the concept of neighbor is a relatively advanced concept and to be outside of the group in primitive terms means in itself to be an enemy. We therefore find in the earliest type of race sense nothing more than this sense of kinship, this sense of what now expresses itself in the proverb[,] "Blood is thicker than water."

The basis of all social organization is upon some sort of kinship; in that sense[, it is clear] that kinship is really at the root of human society. As such[,] it is something which makes us regard race as inseparable from any large collective groupings of people. Now, of course, when civilization has advanced to the stage when the history of groups in their relationship to one another becomes the main thing, the main influence, we arrive at a conception of peoples which, after all, is nothing more than a sense of groups which are construed ethnically. Our historical grouping then transmits some of the [basic] ethnic [feelings, because most] of the earlier historical groups were ethnic groups.

A primitive civilization made its [kinship] naturally, there being very little infusion of new blood[.] Anything large enough to constitute a city or state or tribe had this ethnic relation and was of one kith and kin. It was not, however, until the contacts of people grew to another variety that we have what we [now] know in history as the era of tribal warfare. The era of tribal warfare puts a premium upon blood kinship because any set of people who come into touch with the primitive tribe, without gaining a blood kinship with it must [later] come into their [territory] at peril of extinction or subordination; and the subordination that is traceable to these early contacts of history determines largely what shall be the actual historical groups that we know of as peoples. If you will stop to consider "peoples" as a sort of term that mediates between the [kinship] type and the larger ethnic group, what we mean by "people" in the political sense is simply the large group or collective unity of folk that do more or less have a common consciousness[.] Political it may be, but racial it invariably is in the early stages of civilization. Consequently, the association between race or blood and political organization is fundamental in human society, and people believe, even when there is no blood kinship possible, that to be a member of a political society presupposes, really, blood kinship [or a] blood kinship bond. So much so that they go through elaborate formalities of adoption or incorporation by which one people actually fuses [with another people.] There is regarded to be some kind of transfusion of blood, [really a] transfusion of social blood, the[8] blood [of one group mixing][9] with the blood of [another] group [to form a new] ethnic composition. So that, if, for example, one tribe conquers another and cannot reduce it to an absolute state of servitude, it presumes that a tribal intermarriage has taken place and goes through the formality of a tribal marriage by which every member of one tribe is made kinfellow, brother or sister, with the group that takes them. This practice of wholesale adoption[10] [is the basis of a homogenous tribe, political group, or nation.] The ethnic conception of political groups is based [in] primitive ways and practices, and that ethnic conception has never been displaced in human history. Even today, though the nations are [not] ethnic units, they keep up this as an ethnic fiction, and believe it to be an essential part of the conception of peoples in the political sense. It happens then that[,] as long as groups are in a position to annex other peoples[,] they do so under the idea that either the peoples must come into relationship with them through blood kinship or else they must remain alien even though it is necessary for them to join in the same political [unit. Whether they are part of the nation is] largely determined [by] whether or not they can qualify under this fundamental instinct and social requirement of blood relationship. They are happily adopted if they can claim it and substantiate it, and they are [dominated][11] and made slaves if they cannot.

So dominance, then, is the [other side of the] coin[.] Forceful subjugation of the groups [is][12] characteristic of those people that are most exclusive in their conception of [the] kinship bond[.][13] The people that have the strongest conception of kinship [will be more] warlike and will also determine the practices of race contacts[.] So that really the history of successful contacts not only breeds what we might call "dominant" races, but the "dominant" race becomes the "political" race, the politically [powerful] people who can mold contacts their way. Whereas the people who are lacking in this sense will not only be lacking in the capacities for this kind of racial or political dominance, but [they] will come under the more forceful control of what are political or dominant groups.

Now[14] the conception of "inferior" races or "backward" races and of "advanced" races or "superior" races largely comes from the political fortunes and political capacity of peoples. So that [the][15] people that [have][16] not been successful in acquiring dominance, the people that have not been able to force their group [identity] upon another group, will be called the inferior people[. They] will be called the backward people, even though it may be a historical fact that they have contributed more importantly to the civilization of which they are a part than the people that [have][17] been able to actually make the nominal political conquest and [hold][18] political power. So that the ruling people will be the people who invariably dominate the group, not only dominate the group practically but control the actual class distinctions that may prevail in the group, making almost all of the subordinate status of race flow from their will and their traditions.

For this reason, as you can see, a great deal of what must be condemned scientifically as false race theory is perfectly orthodox and perfectly legitimate from the point of view of history, and history is therefore from this [perspective] bad or false science; just as, for example, good practices may be very false in theory.

One can take no essential issue when a people have been politically successful in what is, after all, [a] naturally human practice of justifying their success in terms of their innate forms. You can see that actual practical dominance would lead to notions of superiority and also to a very firm belief in superiority. So[,] from the point of view of history, the successful group is invariably the superior group, so [that] the race that succeeds and conquers is naturally the better race[.] And these distinctions, if confined to [history,] are not at all objectionable, but when transferred into moral associations and relationships they become invidious. Such a transfer is quite inevitable, so that a people that has been successful, for example, as the Romans were when they succeeded in sapping and undermining Greek civilization[, consider][19] their own civilization superior, when[,] in fact, [as in the case of the Romans,] we now know that it was relatively inferior [to that of the conquered Greeks,] from the point of view of general civilization and culture.

It behooves us then to keep our distinctions in their proper places and with respect to political practices[,] to assume humbly that such [notions as "superiority"] refer only to [the] political fortunes of a group and not to any intrinsic or inherent qualities with reference to social culture.

Now the practices of dominant or ruling groups [are],[20] after all, [what][21] I wish to call your attention [to] this evening. For purposes, largely, of focusing our attention upon what the actual career of a dominating group of people is, I call their dominance imperialistic. I call their practices imperialism, in spite of the fact that not all of them actually have had empires or [have] had what we know as imperial institutions. But an emperor does not make an empire[,] nor [do] imperial [institutions make] imperialistic practices[.] And a great many races are imperialistic that do not constitute themselves formally into empires. Imperialism is, it seems to me, essentially the practical aspect of what one might call "race practice" as distinguished from race theory, and all those peoples that in political life have managed to dominate [the] political life [of other peoples] are imperialistic peoples. This is what we mean when we use the term "imperialism" in these lectures.

There is a broad contrast between this sort of imperialistic practices in the ancient world and the modern world. A good deal of analogy is drawn now in modern days between ancient imperialism and modern, as if one was but the continuation of the other. This does not seem to be so, particularly because the [institutions] of the ancient imperialistic peoples were not so typical of ancient imperialism as is too often thought. Roman institutions, Roman government, was a very complex thing[;] it had many sides to it, and one can get no conception of it merely from, for example, the history of the Caesars. The Romans had in fact several imperial systems. The system in terms of which we now study the Roman Empire was by the Roman, comprehended not so much as one system, but as a[22] group of systems. He would distinguish, as Great Britain today distinguishes, between the colonial system and the imperial system[.] For example, a man says today that he is a subject of the empire and means something quite different from what he would mean by "I am a citizen of a colony." So a man who said, "I am a Roman citizen[,]" would have his statement very differently construed from that of a member of a conquered people in a province[,] a man wholly outside the political institutions of the Roman Empire. So that the Roman Empire as a religious system and political system and a system of tributary government is really three systems instead of one. Now for that reason an account merely of Roman political imperialism will not be at all adequate if we wish to gain a conception of what ancient imperialism really [was.][23] I must refer you, so brief is our time, to adequate accounts of that system, rather than give you any account of it in detail. [I refer you to] Cromer's [*Ancient and Modern Imperialism*] and Beaulieu's [*De la colonization chez les peuples modernes*, both of which] have made wonderful contributions, revolutionary contributions, to our conceptions of the Roman Empire.[24] What I wish to call your attention to, however, is the fact that the Roman imperial practice, particularly as it affected the diverse or alien peoples, was a very catholic and a very broad policy. It was, after all, a policy not of subjugating wholly the people, and not of incorporating them as a social group, but merely of making the group dependent on the Roman Empire governmentally, and of exacting a certain amount of tribute from them. It was largely a tribute-gathering state, by which they buttressed their rather enormous and expensive system of government.

They didn't interfere with the actual life of the people very much and whatever of formal adoption of Roman law and Roman institutions [they demanded] was only formal, and [they] invariably incorporated a good deal of the actual civilization and culture of the group. Their race practice, then, was largely one of race assimilation, and the subjugated culture was invariably absorbed into the Roman culture and Roman institutions.

Modern imperialism, contrasted with ancient imperialism, attempts quite the opposite thing. There is the belief that there can be only one civilization, instead of the ancient belief that there could only be one empire. The ancients were interested in spreading the empire. They didn't care a bit about how much diversity of civilization there might be. In fact, they rather took pride in the number of civilizations which were [included][25] in the empire. Whereas, curiously enough, the moderns believe in one civilization, and the friends of modern imperialistic policies and governments even try stamping out whatever specific and whatever social culture any group may have, and making them adopt, wholesale if possible, the civilization of the group that comes into dominance. So that modern imperialism attempts, as I say, the substitution of its own civilization for that of the subjected civilization. As you can see, this will produce a great many problems which were absolutely foreign and unknown to the Roman Empire, and the success of Roman imperialism has largely been explained in these later days by their tolerance of ancient forms of civilization and customs.

Modern civilization will do well to follow [the Romans], if it were not so committed to the policy to which I [now] turn my attention.

But the cause which really led modern empires to substitute their civilizations for that of [the] groups they conquered was, after all, an economic cause. The fundamental reason why Great Britain wants India to adopt English institutions is because they want Indians to adopt Birmingham cloth and London woolen goods and all [other manufactured] products which England really is willing and anxious to sell to her colonies. It is the economic factors that are fundamental. I do not think they would have tampered with the social institutions in India, or in any quarter of the globe so ruthlessly as they have, had it not been that modern empire depends upon the capacity of developing in the life of the subjugated people a demand for the same articles which are current in the life of the governing folk. And since customs in the financial sense follow a change in manners on the part of the natives, it has been the modern system of tribute-gathering to make an alien civilization adopt the civilization of Europe.

The civilization of Europe, then, thrives, from the imperialistic point of view, upon an economic basis of an adoption of the goods of European civilization through a false imposition of European civilization upon the social life of whatever group may come within its control and influence. The competitive and industrial basis, then, of modern systems has made almost all empires adopt this practice, which was foreign, largely, to ancient empires, namely [that of] insisting that any conquered or subjugated group immediately adopt the dominant civilization of the makers of empire.

I am quite well aware that this, in a sense, will shock your susceptibilities if you have credited empire with a nobler and more ideal cause than this. You may regard the extension of modern empire as the imperialists themselves regard it, as a sort of missionary crusade of the *highest* type of civilization for the enlightenment and upliftment of areas of the world that have not been so fortunate in their problems. I know that there are a great many fine ideal motives both in imperialism and with imperialists, and I know that there is a whole race of people motiv[ated][26] by the imperialism formula and [the] imperialistic ideal[.] [They][27] do not directly benefit their empire and are [neither] political governors [nor] commercial exploiters. They are the missionaries, and you will be somewhat shocked, perhaps, to have me say that missionarism is practically a corollary of modern imperialism. But if you will talk with intelligent and educated members of race groups that have come under modern missionary influence, you will, I think, be quite convinced that there seems in modern life some sort of inevitable connection between the missionary who comes[,] and the trader who comes to supply the missionary[,] and the soldier who comes to protect both the trader and the missionary—and the flag that comes trailing after. In other words, although the missonary is not exactly the advance guard of empire, the same kind of propensities which make modern men reach

out into empire are the propensities which drive the missionary out[.]
And, although the missonary would go out really independent of empire and without any connection with the imperial system, the actual
state of affairs is this: that the modern empire thrives upon the missionary appeal and upon the justification of [empire][28] which comes from[29]
missionarism as the propaganda of the highest type of civilization and
the highest type of religion that has yet been evolved in the world.

Therefore, although they would have been quite innocent in themselves, in connection with the exploitations of modern *imperialism*, the
missionary movement has not been wholly without its ill effects.[30] And
the [worst][31] of these ill effects has been this justification of empire, so
that it seems to have almost divine sanction, as kinghood once seemed
to have a divine sanction. So that really all of the arts of religious
propaganda reinforce the activities of what is really at bottom a commercial exploitation and a commercialized imperialism, particularly because
the missionary efforts, like the imperialistic efforts, stretch out not only
to the ends of the earth[,] but they seem to rejoice in spanning [the
globe and] bridging the most extreme divergency of social culture. It is
the savages whom the imperialists trade upon and it is to the savage, to
the heathen, irrespective of all social distinctions among them, that we
send the missionaries. Consequently[,] there is current [belief in] a sort
of benevolent imperialism—a justification of the exploitation of peoples
which could only have been the product of, I think, the nineteenth
century[.] Because it is so paradoxical that at any other time, when it
had not the commercial basis to justify it, [missionarism][32] could never
have hoped to have the wholesale adoption that it has had. The very
profitableness of empire has made it possible for European civilization
to indulge in missionarism to the extent that it has. If [*missionarism*] had
not been a valuable political and economical practice, [then] imperialism[,] without it, would have either changed its whole tenor or else the
practice would have lapsed.

The missionary attitude, in so far as it has very often and in many,
many places confirmed the invidious racial instincts, is something that
must be very severely criticized, although the criticism costs one considerably.[33] You can see, perhaps, the justice that there is in such a statement if you reflect for a moment [that] invariably, from the point of
view of the missionary attitude, there is the idea of bringing a light into
darkness—the idea of going not to get something, but to give. Fine, as
an ideal, but, in its practical working, amounting to this: "We come to

27

offer you what you yourselves have not. We come to argue upon the basis of a belief in certain religious tenets, to have you adopt wholesale a system of living, [a][34] system of living [which] will revolutionize your culture, and, in fact, rob you of whatever is traditional and whatever is particularly your own in your own culture. More than that, we are superiors. We come to you frankly saying that to you, and we expect you to acknowledge that superiority."

There is in this, particularly when it is complicated by the racial approach, as you can see, the implication of a status of inferiority and a status of dependence and, I am very much afraid, a dominance which is really justified and practiced for political and economic reasons[. My intention is not to disparage] these humanitarian ideals[.][35] It is rather [to unmask][36] a false association between missionarism and imperialism that I take the courage to make these remarks, that I am well aware are not at all popular or not at all likely to find favor.

Now I suppose it may have crossed your minds: "Why should a group of people[,] who themselves are not imperial subjects[,] concern themselves so much with imperialism and imperialistic practice?" I have discerned that attitude on the part of a considerable number of persons with whom I wished to discuss the imperialistic systems with particular reference to racial relations. The idea has been[:] "That may be well and good for people who li[v]e[37] in an empire, but we live in a democracy [and] it doesn't concern us.["] It would concern us even if it did not affect us, because[,] I take it, from the particular point of view [of][38] race contacts and race relationships[,] we should be concerned if over half of the darker peoples of the world live actually in the direct sphere and operation of empire. I should think we ought to be a little concerned, at least to the extent [of understanding] what imperialistic theory really means, and its contact with [diverse] groups of people.

More than that, empire not only concerns us, but affects us. If it were not for the successful imperial practices of one branch of the Anglo-Saxon people, we would not have to confront that attitude on the part of another group of Anglo-Saxons. Because the sense of a dominant race, which really means a race that has learned how to dominate in actual centuries of political and imperial practices[, perpetuates] a sense which never could spring up just from the innate instincts of men. This is something which is confirmed and developed through years of successful political practices, so much so that modern civilization today is largely in the hands and control of peoples that have had centuries of successful imperial practice behind them. And one group of that people professes empire[;] the other group of that people, without an imperial system, has imperial tendencies and the race instincts and feelings that are born of a dominant group. More than that, if empire should lapse, this attitude in viewing governmental and political institutions would also lapse. As long as empire lives, I fancy, that spirit will live in the world.

Now I am not an enemy of imperialism by any means, nor am I a person who expects to see empire vanish in a generation or two. But I am a person who is convinced that there is some connection between the instincts for dominance and the practices of dominance, and I believe that one could not have come about without the other. If they are really cause and effect, then, if we would understand them scientifically, let us study them so.

Anglo-Saxon superiority—which you recognize as a phrase for some of the most virulent conceptions of race in the practical sense—[is][39] a trademark of modern empires as well as the first commandment of modern empire. I don't know if you could realize it without having traveled or lived in contact with a system of empire. This is one point on which I have to ask you, really, to take my experience, as part confirmation. It is the one point about which I shall have to ask you to accept, really, something which I cannot sketch except in terms of my own personal experience. I lived for three years in close association with imperial folk at the "Imperial Training School"[40] at the University of Oxford. Oxford and Cambridge rule the English Empire, and if anything that I shall say regarding empire and imperialistic practices seems farfetched, I fetch it to you from the very seat of the policy.

Some[41] years ago, at the order of U.S. Senator Lodge (then Chairman of the Committee on Foreign Relations), there was compiled by the Librarian of Congress a bibliography of the literature of Anglo-Saxon interests. There are six hundred odd titles of books and articles written to justify and to explain Anglo-Saxon dominance and Anglo-Saxon superiority, and the broadest of those assumes, without a shadow of doubt, the basic idea that Anglo-Saxon dominance *is due* [to][42] Anglo-Saxon superiority, and that Anglo-Saxon superiority is inherent and hereditary, and inherent and hereditary upon the basis of race. It is a literature which is confessedly racial from start to finish. It is an attitude of mind cardinally ethnic in its very conception. More than that, there has been growing among different branches of the Anglo-Saxon peoples a sense of political affinity with the so-called "Mother Race," which is the race which has so successfully molded out of circumstance and fortune, the British Empire. The dominant group in the hegemony of Anglo-Saxon peoples has been the English people. And the English practice of empire has been held up by both historians and practical statesmen as the chief accomplishment of a whole race of people[.] So that if you were to ask them what[43] was their ultimate contribution to civilization, they would have said that it was the way in which they have conquered and dominated more than [half of] the globe [and extended] their institutions over areas that other peoples control. There is common agreement upon the basis of this English policy of empire, because even those who emulate, emulate it because they envy it. European nations—the Germans, the French, the Russians—practically subscribe in theory to the British Imperial policy and practice. Even when they deny it most, they deny it only to affirm its basic principle. Their denial amounts to only this: "It is a fine thing. We only wish we had it." You see that there is really universal agreement in Europe, practically, in this that has really become the dominant system of political organization.[44]

Only a glance at the writings of the leading European statesmen— [whether those who][45] wrote for home consumption [or those who][46] wrote for colonial opinion—confirms us in this statement. Cromer,[47] Morley,[48] Bryce,[49] Clemenceau,[50] Delcasse,[51] Dernberg[52] (in Germany)—all of them voice the same sentiments, and they voice the same sentiments both as practical governors and as social theorists, and try in their social theory to justify what, of course, as exponents of empire[,] they must advocate [in the name of] practical statesmanship. They, too, insist that racial supremacy is the keystone of empire. In other words, they do not see how it is possible for them to dominate except as they force submission to the principle that they are a dominant race—destined, some of them would say, to this position. Others, more modern, would simply say and admit that it was the good fortune of circumstance [that they have power], but would claim that [that] was their just right to the position which they held. In other words, they cannot conceive of empire except upon the basis of the maintenance of this racial superiority.

To go back to the question as to how far it should concern us[:][53] America is substantially not only a supporter but an ally in this joint European policy of race empire. Not only in the flurry of imperialism of 1898 but ever since, there has been an adoption of this policy in American thought and American statesmanship, not essentially as a practice of empire but in the growing sense of ethnic unity and affiliation with the group of peoples who propose not only to dominate the universe but to keep that dominance in their hands. Some of the leading political exponents of American thought believe that the only way in which America will ever gain participation in world politics will be through alliances upon this basis. Every alliance that has been proposed for some time, as well as every broad policy, with the exception of the policy of Pan Americanism, has been along the line of this Anglo-Saxon federation. It has gone so far that just [over][54] a year [ago], a book of considerable circulation and considerabl[y] more significance than the attention that it attracted, was written by Mr. Kennedy on the Pan-Angles.[55] His idea [is][56] that the evolution of race and language should be the basis for an actual political alliance between all of the Anglo-Saxon people, and that for this purpose the Anglo-Saxons who are held in comparative subordination in the English colonies should be[57] incorporated into the maintenance of a policy of racial empire (following the example of the division of South Africa) in order to subjugate more firmly the alien races of the empire, and to draw the distinction already [made] between the imperial domain and the colonies.

This has been a growing feature of British governmental policy ever since 1908. Ever since 1908 the great exponents of English empire have been advocating making concessions to the colonies that were ethnically of the same group with the mother country. They believed that they should be confederated, or rather federated first and confederated after. The Imperial Conference of the year 1908 was predicated largely upon that basis.[58] The representation of alien groups, even though they held the same political status of groups [of Anglo-Saxons was limited in comparison to those Anglo-Saxons] that were represented. [Representation in the conference] was divided [along racial lines,] and association in that conference, which was rather a secret matter, was largely based upon the idea that sooner or later there would have to be within the empire a race confederacy in order to have the empire survive. And the federation of South Africa was the first important and open step toward the realization of the policy that was decided upon in that Imperial Conference held in London.

A book like *The Pan Angles* is simply a reflection of that recent policy and its probable adoption. One reason that I assign for its not attracting much attention is the fact that possibly[,] it is considered to be [the better] part of wisdom not to pay too much attention to what is understood to be the latest phase of British imperial practice. At any rate, the adoption of the policy would seem to depend upon some kind of ethnic confederation or else all nations, the Anglo-Saxon nations in Europe[,] would not be so anxious as they most obviously are to encourage it.[59] The greatest disappointment in Europe was when the United States seemed formally to announce [opposition to] imperialism; and one of the aims of European statesmanship today is to not only convert America but to enlist America into this broad policy of European empire. The common factor of race problems is not in imperial institutions but in the imperialistic temper of the Anglo-Saxon race, which is common to them whether they practice empire or not. But this factor we only could have arrived at, I think, through tracing it in its successful derivation and substantiation through imperial practices. What we know of this [today] as the color-line (I shall have something to say of that in a later lecture, explaining the way in which it appears to have come about) is essentially the line drawn by the practice of what I call commercial imperialism. Commercial imperialism is something which the United States practices as much as Germany[,] or England[,] or France[,] or Russia, although political imperialism is something confined, fortunately, as yet to European practices.

Commercial imperialism means the effort on the part of [Anglo-Saxon nations] to further trade dominance[60] [by] foist[ing] their civilization upon any group having an alien civilization that they can persuade or force to adopt it. If the force of persuasion is [successful,] then the conquest is [primarily on the economic side; if more force is needed, then pressure is exerted] but on the political side[, and] then support [is given] the merchant to the extent of sending the flag and all that goes along with the flag—eventually sending the consuls and proconsuls, and you know, of course, what that [means.]

The reason for so much fear of economic aggression on the part of alien groups in the Orient particularly is simply this: [political dominance usually follows economic relationship.] We[61] see that in the past the Anglo-Saxon races have not separated the practice[62] of commercial imperial[ism] from the practice of political dominance[,] and they believe that the one inevitably follows the other; or else they would not object as they do to economic aggression; and economic aggression would not be aggression at all, but simply exchange, were it not for the circumstance [which] persists among these people for following up any kind of economic relationships with governmental dominance. More than that, I fancy that we lose considerable perspective when we differentiate between what we call the fate of peoples confronting an imperial system and the fate of our group that confronts not an imperial system, but[,] nevertheless, a system of practical racial distinctions and discrimination. Because[,][63] although it would not have been true under ancient conditions, under modern conditions to be subjected to economic subordination and social prejudice is similiar to being subject to political dominance and commercial exploitation. If you li[v]e[64] within the system, you confront what is, after all, the internal or home policy of imperialism. If you live without, you confront what is properly the imperialistic attitude and the imperialistic relationship; but there is very little difference except in the formal way in which you come under it[.] Because, after all, the modern world does not discriminate between a merely political relationship and an economic relationship. In the ancient world[,] there was this distinction: you could be formally a tributary of the Roman Empire and at the same time have another religion, and have, within the imperial system, your own local government. In fact, [you could] keep your own culture rather intact; but both within and without, under modern conditions and in contact with Anglo-Saxon peoples, this seems to be impossible. So that I construe it that it is[,] after all, more or less similar to confront the Anglo-Saxon policies [of][65] race as we do, or to confront them as those who live actually under empire do.

Professor Giddings[66] comes rather to the rescue of this aspect of modern society to which I am calling your attention, by pointing out that[,] after all, modern civilization is of a type calculated to stress the ethnic basis. It may be[67] rather characteristic of most civilizations[,] as I have indicated at the beginning of this lecture, to stress the ethnic basis. But what Professor Giddings means is this: that present day civilization puts a premium upon the group that can convince other groups of its superiority, and that any contact, even economic contact, with such groups is taken to be at least a tacit assumption of such superiority. In other words, the temper of the modern mind has become so confused, it seems[,] that if you will admit that you are economically connected or subordinated to a group, you thereby admit all that they wish to construe further concerning your inferiority and subordination in other matters.

Monsieur Finot also points out the same fundamental [fact of modern life,] although he points it out upon a different basis, what he calls

33

"ethnic concentrations" or "ethnic federations," regarding the conscious reaching out of peoples along ethnic lines as characteristic, uniquely characteristic, of modern politics. It was only the accident, perhaps, of ancient politics that it followed the kinship line. But modern politics consciously follows the kinship line. Greek and Roman colonial practices did to some extent; for example, when they sent out cities into Asia Minor, they maintained a closer relationship between themselves and these colonies than they did in the case of the ones they had conquered.[68] The colony in ancient times had to have a considerable body of actual political [representatives from the home country in order] to establish a particular kind of civilization. But now, as you can see, that is not necessary. Now, instead of sending out colonial groups, all that is needed to make a modern colony is a proconsul and a small army and a corps of bureaucratic administrators. So that we can establish a colony nowadays by merely setting up the flag.

Civilization[69] [is being divided along ethnic lines because] in [a][70] practical way [conflict] follows ethnic lines more [today] than it used to. More today, I imagine, than at any other time, [alliances represent] the actual racial groupings in practical politics. Merely a glance will indicate to you how modern civilization has stressed this ethnic basis[, in such phrases as] Anglo-Saxonism [and] the successive Pan-Slavisms. The immediate issue which touched off the powder barrel in the present war was Pan-Slavism. Because Russia says Austria wished to denationalize Serbia, [and] Austria[, in turn,] wishes to strike Serbia because Serbia is our trump card in the Pan-Slavic policies of the Balkans[. Then there is] Pan-Germanism—you know what that means. And [then] the Pan-Anglian movement, [which,] although a new term, is the original thing under modern times and modern conditions, because it is the policy of the British Empire. And then the counter-movements which have grown up, part[ly] in imitation of, and part[ly] in reaction [to][71] the movements that I have just mentioned—the Pan-Islamic and the Pan-Asiatic [movements.] And even the Pan-Ethiopian movement, feeble as it is, yet nevertheless [fosters] protest against [the imperialistic policies] that the African peoples have had to [endure under European imperialism.]

These tendencies[, dividing civilization along ethnic lines,] are not only uniquely characteristic of modern civilization[,] but they are as yet without any careful explanation. Perhaps our civilization is to be regarded as of the expansive type—expansive to a degree unknown [in] other ages[;] and I, myself, am hoping that really we are at a stage of civilization when such ethnic confederations, when such ethnic crusades[,] are [no longer] necessary[,] and that the expansive type of civilization will not last always[;] and that[,] therefore[,] we need not be alarmed and think that these policies or practices are in themselves so ineradicable.

We shall turn our attention, at the next lecture, to the actual working of these contacts[,] and we shall perhaps see that modern civilization is just at a time in which these [practices] have come to the surface, although it has aggravated [the relations between nations and social groups. The greater awareness today of imperialistic practices][72] may be a sign that [such practices] are about to come to a close. We at least shall have to come to terms with them. Modern society is today fighting to determine, perhaps, who shall have the leadership in this kind of policy, and I shall be very much surprised if the leadership shall not be modified somewhat[.] And I shall be still more surprised, even if the leadership should remain in the same hands, to see the policy remain in exactly the same [hands and be carried out in exactly the same] way in which it has. Empire is[,] at present, as a political state, in a testing furnace, and it undoubtedly will come out something essentially different from what it has been. We scarcely know as yet whether it will be for the better or for [the] worse; we scarcely know how quickly it will be modified or merged. But we do know that as an issue, a world issue of practical politics today, there is in imperialism sufficient [importance] to merit the rather superficial attention which we, perhaps, have been able to give it this evening.

If empire is the political problem of the present day (since empire involves, after all, interracial relations, [and] since the practice of empire has not only been built upon that, but seems to end in it), [then] the bearing of policies of empire upon race questions is undoubtedly very[,] very close[.] I fancy that if we should study race problems from the particular point of view of imperial political practice[, then] we should have an attitude toward them which, at least, would be broader than that which we usually have.

NOTES: LECTURE 2

1. Word deleted following "undertake": "although".
2. Word deleted following "considerations": "which".
3. Word order changed. Original: "and the theory only modern."
4. Clause deleted following "and": "a great many things have had to be taken for granted before we were in a position to know anything about their nature; and".
5. Phrase deleted following "that": "their should be".
6. "operate in" replaces original "pervading".
7. "operate in other societies and" replaces original "should pervade the society of— or".
8. Word deleted following "the": "new".
9. Word order changed. Original: "going in the ethnic composition with the actual blood of the group that makes contact."
10. Word order changed and broken up into two sentences. Original: "This practice of wholesale adoption [.....] what [...] primitive ways and practices [...] the ethnic conception of political groups is based and that ethnic conception has never been displaced in human history."
11. "dominated" replaces original "subjected".
12. "is" replaces original "are".
13. Clause deleted following "bond": "and it works both forward and backward, not only with"
14. Clause deleted following "Now": "although [....] terms of contrast which originally [....] only with theories of race [...] such as we know and are familiar with, as, for example,[...]"
15. "the" replaces "a".
16. "have" replaces "has".
17. "have" replaces "has".
18. "hold" replaces original "the people that has determined within its own limits the succession of what we know as".
19. "consider" replaces original "they considered".
20. "are" replaces original "is".
21. "what" replaces original "the thing to which".
22. Phrase deleted following "a": "sort of".
23. "was" replaces original "is".
24. Evelyn Baring Cromer, *Ancient and Modern Imperialism* (London: John Murray, 1910). The Earl of Cromer (1841–1917) was Britain's Agent and Consul-General in Egypt from 1883 to 1907. As one of Britain's "new imperialists," Cromer sought to contrast Britain's "beneficent intention" in its empire with what he interprets as the less humane and less democratic policies of Rome towards its subjects. Locke obviously saw Britain's paternalism as more pernicious. Pierre Leroy-Beaulieu, *De la colonization chez les peuples modernes*, 2d ed., revised, corrected, and enlarged (Paris: Guillaumin et Cie., 1882). Pierre Paul Leroy-Beaulieu (1843–1917) was the leading conservative French economist of his time, whose *De la colonization chez les peuples modernes* was a popular, well-regarded book. He was also founder of *L'Economiste Français*, in which he advanced the notion that money invested in the Congo would bring greater profit to France than that invested at home. Beaulieu was part of the new wave of colonialists, who, following Britain's example, believed in the economic exploitation of Africa through bureaucratic administration and capital investment rather than war and emigration. (Prosser Gifford and William Roger Louis, eds. *France and Britain in Africa: Imperial Rivalry and Colonial Rule* (New Haven and London: Yale University Press, 1971), 23–25, 184.)

25. "included" replaces original "comprehended".

26. "motivated" substituted for original "motived".

27. "They" replaces original "but [...]".

28. "empire" replaces original "it".

29. Phrase deleted following "which comes from": "the justification of it...."

30. Paragraph break inserted at beginning of the sentence.

31. "worst" replaces original "largest".

32. "missionarism" replaces original "it".

33. Paragraph break inserted at beginning of the sentence.

34. Word order changed. Original: "which system of living".

35. Word deleted following "ideals": "and".

36. "to unmask" replaces original "in the unmasking of".

37. "live" replaces original "life".

38. Word order changed. Original: "from the particular point of view [...] we should be concerned in race contacts, and race relationships: and if over-half of the darker peoples of the world live, actually in the direct sphere and [...] operation of empire."

39. "is" replaces original "as".

40. Quotation marks added around Imperial Training School. Here Locke refers to his years at Oxford University as a Rhodes Scholar from 1907 to 1910 and not to any specific "Imperial Training School."

41. Word order changed. Original: "There was compiled some years ago at the order of Senator Lodge, then Chairman of the Committee on Foreign Relations, by the Librarian of the Library of Congress, a bibliography of the literature of Anglo-Saxon interests." The bibliography Locke refers to is *Select List of References on Anglo-Saxon Interests*, compiled by Appleton Prentiss Clark Griffin, Chief Bibliographer, Division of Bibliography, Library of Congress (Washington, D.C.: Government Printing Office, 1903). A second issue with approximately twice as many references was issued in 1906. While this bibliography may have been compiled on orders from the enormously influential Senator Henry Cabot Lodge, as Locke suggests, the prefatory note states that the list was compiled in response to requests by letter.

42. "to" replaces original "of".

43. Word deleted following "what": "it".

44. Phrase deleted from the end of the sentence: "from the point of view of [...] group".

45. "whether those who" replaces original "that class which they".

46. "or those who" replaces original "and that class which they".

47. All those cited by Locke supported Joseph Chamberlain's policy of "constructive imperialism," with its concern for attracting capital to the colonies and its denial of colonial self-rule for nonwhite colonials on racial grounds. Eveleyn Baring Cromer (1841–1917) was consul-general for Egypt from 1883 to 1907 and the major architect of English policy towards the Egyptians before the war. Cromer, a paternalist, believed that if Egyptians were well-treated, honestly managed, and taxed at a low rate, they would prefer English rule over self-rule. This was because the "oriental mind," as Cromer called it, was unsuited to democratic institutions: Cromer felt that "it will probably never be possible to make a Western silk purse out of an Eastern sow's ear." (Bernard Porter, *The Lion's Share: A Short History of British Imperialism, 1850–1970* (London: Longman's, 1975), 184.)

48. Viscount John Morley (1838–1923), secretary of state for India 1905–1910, followed a similar policy in India, endeavoring to increase Indian cooperation with British rule under a Liberal Government. Morley increased Indian participation in the government, but never possessed any "intention or desire to attempt the transplantation of European form of representative government to Indian soil" (Porter, *The Lion's Share*, 219).

49. Viscount James Bryce (1838–1922), was a brilliant Scottish historian, and author of several books, most notably *The American Commonwealth* (1888), who was most important as an English liberal statesman, serving in the House of Commons, the House of Lords, and in a variety of posts in foreign affairs. That liberalism was effective in his advocacy of the Armenian cause, especially after 1896, when the increased massacres of Armenians led him to public protest and the compilation of information. But Bryce was less effective in promoting a humane imperial policy in Ireland. As a member of the House of Commons, he voted and then regretted his support for the Coercion Bill of 1881 and its denial of the Irish right to self-government. Then, from 1905 to 1907, as chief secretary of Irish affairs, Bryce refused to support immediate recinding of the Coercion Act and also refused, under the influence of his under secretary, Sir Antony MacDonnell, to advance a plan for Irish home rule. Isolated from Irish leaders and unable to act against the larger interests of English imperial rule in Ireland, Bryce left the post in 1907 to become ambassador to the United States. (*Dictionary of National Biography 1922–1930*, edited by J. R. H. Weaver (London: Oxford University Press, 1937), 127–33.)

50. Georges Clemenceau (1841–1929), French prime minister from 1906–09, and 1917–20, denounced colonial expeditions as a betrayal of human rights while a deputy but favored overseas conquest once he became prime minister. Clemenceau dealt with the contradiction between his liberal views and his nation's policy of colonialism by becoming a convert to Social Darwinism. According to Clemenceau, "in this ruthless struggle for existence carried on by human society, those who are weaker physically, intellectually, or morally must in the end yield to the stronger. The law is hard but there is no use in rebelling." He expressed skepticism that black people could survive in competition with whites, observing that "'time alone can show of what the Black race is capable.'" (William B. Cohen, *The French Encounter with Africans: White Response to Blacks, 1530–1880* (Bloomington:Indiana University Press, 1980), 249.)

51. Theophile Delcasse (1852–1923), was the French foreign minister from 1898 to 1905. Prior to that appointment, Delcasse was the under secretary of state for the colonies, having taken charge of the French colonies in January 1893. Although Delcasse's public policy was to put an end to the "military period" and promote commerce, agriculture, and public works in the colonies, most of his tenure in office was spent defending France's claims in Siam, Dahomey, and the Sudan. Delcasse dealt with native resistance in Dahomey by driving out the indigenous chief, Behanzin, but made some efforts to respect ancient laws and institutions of the Dahomey in order to maintain French control. (Alan Palmer, *Who's Who in Modern History, 1860–1980* (New York: Holt, Rinehart, and Winston, 1980), 101–2, Charles W. Porter, *The Career of Theophile Delcasse* (Westport, Conn.: Greenwood Press, 1975), 75–99.)

52. Bernhard Dernberg (1865–1937) was the best example of what Locke described as the "commercial imperialist" who believed that well-run African colonies were the key to a modern nation's economic and political development. Dernberg was a banker, who became secretary of state for Germany's colonies in 1906 and instituted widespread reforms in Germany's colonial administration. Realizing that a paternalistic policy toward Africans would be more profitable for Germany than violence and intimidation, Dernberg instituted programs of western education to "civilize" the natives and to turn them into the best consumers of German manufactured goods. Dernberg was also a good example of how other Europeans imitated English imperial practice: he reorganized German colonial administration along British lines, attracted quality officials with pay increases and benefits, and used his financial connections to build one of the largest colonial railway networks in Africa. As did Chamberlain, Dernberg painted a rosy picture of Germany's colonies in order to attract investment, while he instituted reforms. Dernberg succeeded in making Germany's colonies profitable for the first time. (Evans Lewin, *The Germans*

and Africa (London: Cassell and Co., Ltd., 1939), 315–322; L.H. Gann & Peter Duignan, *The Rulers of German Africa, 1884–1914* (Stanford, Calif.: Stanford University Press, 1977), 53–55, 182–88.)

53. Sentence order of paragraph changed. Original: "To go back to the question as to how far it should concern us. Not only in the flurry of imperialism of 1898 but ever since, there has been an adoption of this policy in American thought and American statesmanship; not essentially as a practice of empire but in the growing sense of ethnic unity and affiliation with the group of peoples who propose not only to dominate the universe but to keep that dominance in their hands. America is substantially not only a supporter but an ally in this joint European policy of race empire."

54. "over" replaces original "above".

55. Sinclair Kennedy, *The Pan-Angles: A Consideration of the Federation of the Seven English-Speaking Nations* (New York and London: Longmans, Green and Co., 1914). The Pan-Angles are "English-speaking whites who are the self-governing forces in the Seven" English-speaking nations: New Zealand, Australia, South Africa, Newfoundland, Canada, the British Isles, and the United States (28, 81).

56. "is" replaces original "being".

57. Word order changed. Original: "following the example of the division of South Africa—incorporated...."

58. Locke is probably referring to the Imperial Conference of 1907 (there was no conference in 1908) at which the distinction was made between the "colonies," which were nonwhite, non-self-governing, and nonmembers of the Imperial Conference and the "'self-governing Dominions beyond the seas,'" who were white, voting members of the conference. (W. K. Hancock, *Survey of British Commonwealth Affairs. Vol. I: Problems of Nationality, 1918–1936* (London: Oxford University Press, 1937), 47.) The first imperial conference had been held in 1887, an attempt by the colonial secretary on the occasion of the Queen's jubilee to head off increasing demands for a Political Federation to replace the empire. Canada and Australia demanded that something akin to partnership replace an increasingly outworn notion of their colonial subordination to British policies. Chamberlain supported the conferences, especially the Conference of 1902, as a means to promote imperial patriotism; the dominions sought a means to achieve "imperial preference" in trade with England. The conference formula survived because of the sense of growing equality between the "colonies" and the "mother country," and yet the reluctance of Britain to alter formally the imperial relationship. The sticking point, however, in the aftermath of the Conference of 1907 was, what should be done about India? Since the Conference of 1907 recognized the principle of one government, one vote among the dominions, to admit India conferred, at least at the conference, the right of self-government on India, and by extension, to all of the nonwhite colonies. In 1917 India was admitted, although only after considerable protest. At the time that Locke was giving these lectures in 1915 and 1916, the two policies of dominion representation and colonial nonrepresentation in the Empire were being maintained. (Hancock, *Survey,* 28–30, 40–41, 45–50; Porter, *The Lion's Share,* 239–40. I thank Professor Jeffrey Butler of Wesleyan University for bringing these sources to my attention.)

59. Irretrievable sentence deleted following "it": "The United States [...] but has no foreign policy or thought [....] into this practice or into this system."

60. Irretrievable phrase deleted following "dominance": "[...] and used [...] of the desire, at any cost, to".

61. Syntax changed. Original: "We cannot see that the Anglo-Saxon races have in the past separated".

62. Phrase deleted following "practice": "political dominance of ".

63. Phrase deleted following "Because": "after all under modern conditions".

64. "live" replaces "life".

65. "of" replaces original "or".

66. See Franklin Henry Giddings's *Democracy and Empire, With Studies of Their Psychological, Economic, and Moral Foundations* (New York: The Macmillan Co., 1900).

67. Phrase deleted following "be": "although I think it".

68. Sentence order changed and words dropped following "conquered." Original: "But now, instead of sending out colonial groups, all that is needed to make a modern colony is a proconsul and a small army and a corp of bureaucratic administrators. So that we can establish a colony now-a-days by merely setting up the flag. The colony in ancient times had to have a considerable body of actual political [...] to establish a particular kind of civilization, but now, you can see, that is not necessary."

69. Word deleted following "Civilization": "theories".

70. "a" replaces original "the".

71. "to" replaces original "from".

72. "the relations between nations and social groups. The greater awareness today of imperialistic practices" replaces original "[....] shows whether civilization [...] as well as [...] world over".

3

The Phenomena
and Laws
of Race Contacts

I N PASSING to the phenomena and laws of race contacts, we pass to
that phase of the subject which confronts us with conditions as
they are[.][1] In this lecture,[2] we shall now endeavor to turn our
attention to those conditions which are working today, even though
they may be centuries old. We want to try to record those forces that are
invariable phenomena of racial contacts and we want also to see if in
investigating these phenomena[,] we [can][3] catch their drift or tendency. Our effort isn't to find a [natural] law, [that is,] to arrive by very
hasty generalization at anything which might be construed as law, but
simply to observe as calmly and dispassionately as we can, the phenomena attendant upon race contacts.

If some of these phenomena should prove to be more or less invariable under similar conditions, we, of course, will be justified scientifically in assuming that we have come into sight of some law of social
relationship. We must have ever in mind, all along, that we must approach the subject without prejudice.

A rather famous scientist, who was a bacteriologist, was conducting a
visitor through his laboratories and was very surprised to see the [visi-
tor's] natural, instinctive recoil from the germ cultures that he was
exhibiting and explaining[.] And being a great scientist, he said: "It is
absolutely necessary in science that one should neither love nor hate,
dread nor admire," meaning[4] that it would absolutely vitiate one's science to have any preconceptions towards the conditions and phenom-

ena which he expected to see. The scientific eye sees impartially and it tries to see the object as it is in itself. Now, if there has been anything that has hindered the observation of the phenomena of race contacts it has been that unscientific point of view which has colored, favorably or unfavorably, the facts so that it has been almost impossible to extract any clear scientific attitude or scientific result from the process. It isn't that we haven't had considerable observation of the actions and reactions of social [groups,] but because so much of it has been prejudiced, favorably or unfavorably[,] that so much must be discarded as essentially unscientific and as not aiding the situation one way or another.[5]

You will notice that the bibliography under this heading is extremely small, smaller than the bibliographies under any other head.[6] The actual works are, as a matter of fact, more numerous under this caption than under any other, but I have tried to discard all that have been colored [by propaganda and to include only those which approach the subject] from the scientific point of view[.] Because if we are to arrive at anything in this lecture[,] it is [a] dispassionate account of the way in which race groups react to one another in their presence together under the same forms of society or social organization.

I should like at this point to call your notice to the fact that in this lecture we try to be quite objective[.] We permit ourselves in the lecture that is to come, to criticize certain of these reactions and frankly to speak of failures[,] implying that we shall judge, implying that we shall discriminate; and yet, as a preliminary to that, it seems absolutely necessary that we should have this dispassionate attitude.[7]

Now, an impartial and dispassionate study of race contacts seems to me to be the only scientific basis for the comprehension of race relations. You can say that this would be obviously so, and it seems so strange that with the modern scientific temper it has been so often overlooked[.] Because here we have in the actual conditions prevailing in various social groups what, after all, must be regarded as the scientific data for any theory that we may later have concerning the nature of society, the nature of its reactions between its several component groups.

This is an important phase of social study and for us important far beyond any consideration of race relationships, because the same tendencies which separate class groups (and groups other than class groups) in society, will be identical with those that affect the racial groups. So that a systematic study of race contacts will teach us a great deal con-

cerning the actual nature of human society. It is more important, perhaps, for the broad general study of human society than it is from its
bearing upon merely the "race question," as it is called.

But so many people mistake this attitude which one should have,
with the attitude of the historian. Now a history of race contacts would
be interesting, and yet that is not what we propose in this lecture. The
history of race contacts is history, and we should never confuse history,
as an account of social reactions, [with][8] that more scientific approach
to it which we have today in the so-called economic and sociological
sciences. We wish to study race reactions so that we may know how it is
that one group in society reacts in a certain way toward another group.
And from that point of view, it seems, racial contacts offer, as I have
said, one of the most fruitful fields for sociological observation and
research and promise to give us some real clue concerning the actual way
in which human beings behave in groups. A[9] behavioristic account of
the way in which human society constitutes itself and divides itself and
subdivides itself and then unites and re-unites is what we are after in
approaching the subject of the phenomena and the laws of race
contacts.

We[10] study human society in the same way in which the biologist
studies and observes life forms. [The social scientist] tries to find out
from the very behavior of the component parts what it is that in society,
functioning normally and abnormally, constitutes these actions and reactions. I want to emphasize here the analogy between this kind of
sociological science and biology, because, as you know, the progress of
biological science has been largely through the observation of the abnormal or unusual. Pathology has established curative bacteriology—that
has been the glory and justification of the first era of pathological investigation. And always the study of the abnormal seems to establish what
is really normal. If we regard certain of the reactions of race contacts as
abnormal phenomena in society, perhaps, in society, we not only gain a
scientific notion of what they themselves are, but gain in addition a
knowledge of what the normal functional reactions of human society
are and should be. In the light of the abnormal, the normal constitutes
itself. So that really in the study of some of the phenomena of race
contacts[,] there is an opportunity for the soundest notion of what
human society *is* functionally.

In confronting these phenomena, there are certain dangers, certain
obvious dangers[,] to be evaded. There is, in the first place, the danger

of merely construing everything which happens under these conditions to be invariable and in itself a law[.] The danger of erecting phenomena into laws is not a peculiar danger, perhaps, to this subject, [although][11] I fancy it is a danger into which a great many otherwise competent observers have fallen. They have succumbed to the obsession that everything which happens is the invariable rule. Consequently[,] we have some of the most absurd generalizations, generalizations which discourage [investigation] and have discredited the [scientific] attempt which should have been made constantly to observe society from this point of view.

I fancy we shall have to mediate between one of two rather natural and yet very dangerous positions, the one regarding race contacts as wholly automatic, and the other regarding them as wholly deliberate. They span both the voluntary and the involuntary actions of peoples in groups. Consequently[,] we must not arbitrarily say that all of these practices and conditions are automatic and beyond means of control[,] and we should not, on the other hand, claim that they are all deliberate and thus within man's control[.] Because some of them are undoubtedly automatic and instinctive with individuals and with groups, and others are quite within the range of the individual will and the collective will, as well as within the range of the deliberate function of human beings in society. Race problems, if you will pardon the first interjection of that rather objectionable [phrase],[12] race problems constitute themselves largely out of the groupings, the larger social groupings, which seem caused by racial differences or what we would say [is] the ethnic sense of one group as contrasted with the ethnic sense of another group. We somehow or other regard race feeling and the kind of group relationship and feeling which we call "racial" or "ethnic" as different in kind from the same kind of group feeling which prevails in what we know as social classes. I fancy that is the fundamental mistake, because, however extreme they may be and seemingly different, race feelings (group sense that moves on racial lines) is only different in degree and not different in kind from class sense and class groupings. In fact[,] there are some class groupings and feelings that are just as radical, just as arbitrary, and just as violent as racial feelings.

Several instances were cited to me in correspondence with a school friend[13] who is now teaching in a midwestern university,[14] which convinced me that there were instances of class feeling which were more violent, more instinctive, and more inhibitive, than what we know [of] as the most violent kind of race feeling.

So we must constantly stress the analogy between race issues and class problems or race problems and class problems, race feelings and class feelings, as you will regard them as really of the same kind and different only in degree and only according to[15] the basis upon which they are practiced.

Now all such problems and issues originate, after all, not in the mind, but in the practical problems of human living. Men in groups do not always get along well together. And even when they apparently would get along quite well but for certain obstacles, it seems that it is the nature of human society to generate those obstacles. Civilization isn't a smooth course. Civilization very often produces counter-currents. Civilization is something which in itself seems to involve very often these rough places, these antagonisms, these struggles, these actions and reactions, because the reactions are, after all, just as inevitabl[y] part of the process, it seems, as the positive actions themselves. So that wherever we find groups amalgamating in society, we must expect to find groups differentiating and separating out. It is really, after all, one side of the same tendency; and I think the thing which separates people into groups is functionally, in human society, the same thing which brings them together in groups. If the consciousness of kind unites, the consciousness of kind must separate. There is a sort of logic in human society. There is sociological logic, which Professor Cobb was the first to call very favorably to our attention, which seems to necessitate this action and reaction, this thesis and antithesis, this contrary result of the same principle or tendency.[16]

So really, we must not regard these phenomena apart from normal phenomena, no more than the biologist today regards the inimical bacteria differently from those that are helpful. In fact, a bad bacterium is very often a good bacterium gone wrong, and a deadly culture is very often an antitoxin—the curative agent in the modern art of healing. So[,][17] I think that we must confront without prejudice these reactions and tendencies in human society, [and] look at them, as the scientist would look at them, as simply evidences of the way in which human beings act and react when they are in groups.

Now, of course, as early as the dawn of history, we see what we would call group feeling prevailing[,] and within groups[—even within societies—] that from the point of view of government, from the point of view of culture, from the point of view really of all the essential larger structures, the society was one. So that we see no social unit so small that it hasn't itself subdivisions, that it hasn't its classes, that it hasn't its groups, that it hasn't within itself some more or less contradictory elements.

In the earliest times, these contradictory elements were largely those of class and they were construed as differences of class, or in ancient society, differences of caste, even when they actually amounted to racial differences.

The closest scrutiny of the earlier kinds of grouped differences in human society show[s] them to have been largely practical and economic in their derivation. So that even when they did run parallel to what was fundamentally a racial difference, the difference *was not apprehended* [as][18] racial difference but *as* a caste or class difference. So that when we see that largely the castes in India follow ethnic lines we are apt to be misled and think that they are racial in origin. As a matter of fact[,] the castes in India have produced races rather than [having][19] arisen out of races. They started largely as economic differentiations, class differences, caste differences, but because they were enforced by a strict [social code,] by strict marriage laws, they have practically resulted in racial differences[.] So that in the East today a caste represents a race, practically, a difference of blood, but originally they represented a difference of occupation and a difference, as we would call it, of class.

Now, of course, the earlier societies were very arbitrary [in their governing of] life, and it is not surprising to us that we find very arbitrary regulations dealing with the relationships of people who belonged to different castes in early society.[20] Half of the social code of primitive societies concerns itself with governing the relationships of individuals, prescribing what they shall and shall not do [in][21] relation to individuals of a different caste or of different tribes. The tribal difference and the caste difference seem [to be] almost identical[.] So that, for example, just as severe penalties and restrictions are put upon association of one kind or another with members of different castes [as] are put upon relationships with members of alien tribes; and the first distinctions which alienat[e] men seem rather to grow up *as much* within societies [as][22] from the contact of societies with other groups.

And yet[,] in spite of all this arbitrary social prescription by code of the relationships between one individual and another[,] because that individual belonged to one caste and the other individual belonged to an opposite or different caste, [there] is something which we can trace [that is][23] very fundamentally human. It seems arbitrary. It is arbitrary.

It is counter really to the instinctive actions of people; and yet primitive religion, primitive society, in all of its institutions, seems to rest fundamentally upon some *such* [counter][24] tendency which shall keep people from following the natural tendencies which would lead to complete assimilation and absorption.

Some of the best and most representative products of civilization seem in the beginning to have been vitally at stake in these regulations. For example, I question whether we should have developed certain very useful classes in society had it not been for the law which says, "The man who does this must keep to himself. The man who does this is a better man than the man who does that." It puts a premium upon certain types, and the types upon which the premiums are put develop, and by developing[,] lead to distinctive cultural tendencies in those societies, so that it may seem that the perpetuation, the hereditary perpetuation[,] of privilege is in itself vital to the early types of civilization. So that [race distinction is] after all, [nothing] but the perpetuation of class [distinction] as a heredity of caste. No one can question the advantages of that kind of a regime in the early stages of human social organization. Consequently[,] we see that although it is seemingly natural for what we might call [social osmosis or] natural assimilation (natural mixing) [to take place,] it is very fortunate [for] human contacts [that the opposite tendency exists.] All of the fundamental tendencies of earlier civilizations are counter tendencies to [assimilation] and run against the current of the natural instincts of human beings. So much so[,] that the civilized human being has[25] these distinctions ingrained in his disposition[26] by centuries of heritage. The distinctions are not harmful in themselves, but harmful only as they are unjustly perpetuated or irrationally practiced. And yet, there is a strange paradox to be observed at this stage, because if any one is really interested in what we might call just mere perpetuation of race, or class, or caste for its own sake, he would, he should insist, according to the actual answer of history, not upon violent caste or racial distinctions but rather upon the opposite[.] Because it has been out of the social inequalities of peoples that actual blood assimilation has transpired, rather than out of their equalities.

One of the hasty ways to amalgamate a people is to make slaves of them. One of the most contradictory ways of suppressing[,] really[,] the sense of blood or of class is to enforce it rigidly. Because[,] in the first place[, suppression] develops the desire on the part of one group to become like the other group and to gain its privileges. And in the second place[,] it actually facilitates (under most systems of which we have been observers) blood intermixture, which is, of course, the final way in which such tendencies seem to be counteracted. So that [self-] preservation of this kind seems to be a first law of human society, the preservation at which class and caste and rigid racial sense really aim[. Yet it] is a preservation which, after all, the *course of human events* contradict. The way in which rigid code distinctions have contradicted themselves in the course of human history is rather amusing to an impartial and unprejudiced observer. One of the virtues of this unprejudiced attitude is to see the way in which time after time, in one society after another, the arbitrary holding of such caste distinctions has brought about their own downfall and contradiction.

Yet, to turn to specific matters (because we want, if possible[,] to arrive at some definite scientific observation of the way in which race and class groups react toward one another in society), I fancy the most reliable clue [to race relations in society] is that of restricted status. Because whenever such a sense develops in human society, one of the first things that happens is for one group to attempt to restrict, or define at least, the status of the other group. Sometimes this definition of status comes from both sides, and we have the phenomena that we see in the [Far] East where, so to speak, to use a plain phrase, the groups "stick out their tongues at one another." There is just as much dislike and antipathy on one side as on the other. But more generally, we have in the definition of status, the initiative, at least, taken by the group that construes itself to be more important (or by the group which can construe itself as more important), that is the group which is, for the time being, dominant. So that the restriction of the status of other groups by the dominant groups, whether they be class groups or race groups, is the invariable phenomena in this kind of group federation in society.

Now, the earliest forms of this restricted status were brought about, possibly, by legal restriction. It is dangerous to make this assertion without the opportunity of going into a great deal of the historical evidence, and yet[,] if without doing so I can convince you that it is the consensus of the best historical opinion that the conditions are[27] caused by legislation rather than [being][28] the effects registered in legislation, [then] I shall have brought to you what is really the first scientific law that we [now] come in sight of. It is difficult to say, really, which comes first—the actual difference which registers itself in law, written or unwritten, or whether the law, the custom itself, produces and often creates the distinction and the difference.

It would seem, however, that in the majority of instances, almost as soon as there is any recognition or sense of a difference, the law springs up to help confirm it and perpetuate [the difference].[29]

One of the saddest phenomena with which the study of society can concern us is the way in which every legal, every customary, prescription accentuates and perpetuates differences [and] handicaps which would perhaps pass off as mere temporary accidents if they did not have the sanction and the perpetuation of the legal or the customary forms. [This is the] *stereotyping function of the law*.[30]

Now, early society was very broad in these matters. They had any number of codes and customs by which restricted status of one kind or another was defined and enforced. The later practices are largely political and economic, but they are invariably legal so that a man's status, his class status, is absolutely prescribed and fixed in most ancient societies. It would require a law, or an enactment by a legislative authority, to transfer a man from one class to another.

A[31] man, for example, [might] pass automatically from [being] a poor man to [becoming] a rich man by the acquisition of money. After getting his million dollars, he would perhaps apply for legislation to get into another class and be legally enacted into that class[, because] his million dollars would not [automatically] get him into the other class.

Early civilizations insisted upon the legal definition of status because they emphasized rigidly the hereditary basis. Any change of status must necessarily be a form change, because [such transformation is] so extraordinarily difficult to make.

Now, we like to think that the position of the slave is the basic position in that ladder, in that social ladder, which the very thought of race itself suggests to us. It is the bottom rung[,] so to speak. We are somewhat in error there, because although all early societies had their practices of slavery and upheld, or at least fell into the institution of slavery, they did not always consider the slave status as the lowest social status. In certain [societies,] it was easier to come into the more respectable grades of society through the status of the slave than through certain others. Early society in fact is characterized by several kinds of restricted status, all of which are today lumped under the head of the status of slavery. In fact, they scarcely knew what slave status was in our sense of "slave status." The early slave was a household slave, and a household slave is invariably a person who must assimilate the culture of the dominant class. *This has worked to a certain extent in America* [because social] *isolation in personal service is impossible.*[32] Consequently[,] the position of the slave in many ancient societies is infinitely better than the position, for example, of the small craftsman, the helot, or the serf who tills the soil. We must regard slavery, the position of the helot, the position of the serf[33] [and the household slave,] as all of them ways in which ancient society divided itself arbitrarily into class groups, some of which were racial groups as well, but all of which were construed more or less according to the class grouping[34] rather than the racial [grouping]. [T]here[35] was more class sense and less race sense in the early societies, [especially among][36] the early [maritime] peoples, because they were very heterogeneous people and[37] [economic] conditions [forced them] to adjust themselves quickly [to] race differences and differences of physical type.

Now, although all of these practices favored early society and [although] we like to think of them as influences which do not pertain to modern society, there is practically none of them which is extinct in modern society—except slavery itself. Slavery is inoperative under modern conditions. On the other hand[,] there is still in the social practices of the world a great deal of the arbitrary limitation of status of peoples by class and by race groups, sometimes under the most enlightened form of government.

We have in our own country a considerable practice of peonage, which is, of course, helotage in a sense. We have in our own country, for example, the sequestration of whole groups of people upon reservations, as for example the treatment of the Eskimo and the Indians upon the western reservations. Peonage and helotage[38] on reservations[,] communal ownership of tribes[, and] private tenure [are still the governmental policy, under which even] property owning and holding [are][39] recognized[.] In fact, wherever society confronts an intractable group that doesn't yield to the institutions and [to] the general social practices, the tendency is to get them off in a corner somewhere and by a mere form of government protection which guarantees to them no governmental [participation]—scarcely a delegate representative sometimes[.] They are put off to themselves and simply governed as a group area[.] Between that [excluded group] and the main body of society[,] there is practically no vital relation[,] no social relation at all.

There are considerable numbers of other groups which are not[40] treated so simply[,] because they are economically indispensable to society. The Negro belongs largely to this group. Certain types of Jews in European countries belong also to this group. And because their presence is economically necessary, they are living actually inextricably mixed with the society of which they are not quite component parts in a social sense. We[41] have a policy practiced in the Middle Ages in European civilization[,] but which was originated in Asiatic societies from time immemorial, of dealing with them in sequestered residence quarters[, such as] the Kraal,[42] and for the city districts, the Ghetto—the legalized Ghetto.[43] I mean [that] the prescribed and restricted residence area is the way in which such groups are largely dealt with by the societies of which they are economically component parts, but of which they are not socially component parts.

Now the very citation of such [restricted] status proves to you that there is still a great deal of race and class practice which is essentially in a very elementary and primary stage and which seemingly has not progressed very far from similar usages in the most primitive kinds of society. [I want] to emphasize that, not in a condemnatory way[,] but simply to call your attention to the fact that there is a great deal of what one might call "lumps" in society[.] And that society which seems to be economically and structurally organic, very economically and structurally organic,[44] is very often not incorporated. [When] groups which must live in it are constituted [as] in one way or another to be necessary to the life of society [and yet are nevertheless forced to live under restricted status, then][45] that human society[,] even under the most enlightened government and under the most modern institutions[,] isn't wholly socialized [and] isn't wholly organized—[it] is still in a position where there is a great deal of internal organization yet to be brought about[,] and really a great deal of the life of the constituent elements of the society is not functional at all in certain respects.

Now the reason why we flatter ourselves so much as modern [people and gloat] upon the differences between ourselves and ancient society is simply that we overlook these facts.[46] [We overlook that our race and class practice has scarcely progressed beyond those practices of primitive societies, that we still sequester groups of people on reservations and in ghettos, and that consequently, our society remains disorganized.] We overlook these facts for a certain very definite reason, a reason which I will cite as a very natural one[:] because modern society has developed an instinct for insulating itself, that is to say, for ignoring social facts. The modern social mind is more tolerant of certain social facts than any other society that has ever existed. [The modern social mind][47] can absolutely live in the presence of a thing and seemingly ignore it, in a way which does not seem characteristic of ancient societies. Ancient societies not only knew their laws but [also] their conceptions[;] but modern society is very instinctive about its laws[, and][48] has codes [that are operative even in the absence of legal restrictions. Such social facts][49] do not seem to influence, really, the social mind at all. Consequently[,] we see this very characteristic modern disavowal of legal disabilities, in which they seem to flout and contradict social facts by simply refusing to recognize them formally, and they say [that] because they have no legal disabilities, disabilities do not exist.

There was a great deal of [confusion,] for example[,] over the abolition of the institution of slavery [in this country] long before the institution of slavery was abolished. [For example,] states [that were merely] in the [process of] putting abolition gradually in force, and therefore still practicing slavery, would consider themselves non-slaveholding states, and consider themselves as members of the northern anti-slavery group.[50] Consequently[,] we see this broad distinction between ancient and modern society on this point. Social distinctions rather than legal or political distinctions are more characteristic of modern society, because, I think, legal distinctions are repellant on the whole to the modern social mind, to the modern conscience. And yet wherever we find the absence of the older kind of political and legal restriction of status, we find a considerable amount of the social restriction, the restriction of social status; and wherever legal and political disabilities are removed or changed suddenly, we find a sudden intensifying of the social distinctions.

We are today, for example, living in a period and in [a] society that has intensified its social distinctions as a reaction [to][51] the removal of certain political and legal disabilities with which you are familiar. Now there is a constant change going on by which not only old groups are fading out, but new groups are being formed; and then while we have the same kind of antagonisms [operating] within society[,] the actual constituency of groups is in the process of change. Consequently[,] while [the intensity of feeling about a] class issue or race problem[52] may change and pass through many phases, it is important to know in which phase it actually is at any particular time. There seems to be a sort of periodicity by which class or racial feelings wax and wane, grow violent and then fade out again. The periodicity of racial antagonisms and class antagonisms (I am invariably speaking of both race and class matters throughout this lecture) is a matter which has been generally observed and admitted[,] but a matter that has not as yet been reduced to a scientific basis. We do not understand just how it is that these things vary, but we do know that they vary. Perhaps in time we shall be able, through broad comparisons and close observation, to trace some kind of law which will state the way in which they vary. We are at least far enough toward a scientific understanding of them that we have noticed the variation.

Now adjustment in society, coming about, as it has to very often, by legal enactment, in itself generates violent changes[.] And a violent change in one direction is apt to be followed by a reaction[,] so that a sort of series of waves[,] on the one hand[,] of moral reform, and[,] on the other hand[,] of social reaction, seem inevitable under most conditions. Now this artificial variation may be different from the "natural periodicity[,]" as we might call it, of the race or class feeling, so that it complicates the situation somewhat because we never have a situation free for any considerable length of time from legislative adjustments[.] It is a very difficult problem to figure out the periodicity of race or class feeling, and what is the actual change from decade to decade, [because] as social conditions are modified[,] certain forms are adopted. Nevertheless[,] this remains to be studied closely, particularly because there is on this point one of the most hopeful deductions, I think, to be drawn in this whole course of studies.

Wherever there is variability there seems to be what I call a margin of social control.[53] People have absolutely no excuse for regarding phenomena as if beyond their control, if the phenomena vary. That may seem strange because the variation in itself may be automatic; but consider that the variation of plants, for example, is a variation of nature. We cannot actually change a plant[;] and yet[,] although we cannot change plant tendencies, by watching the changes and variation in plant tendencies and taking advantage of them we can actually [effect a] cross between two species and thereby get a third species and from that another subspecies and so on. In other words[,] horticulture—although it doesn't change plant growth at all—by taking advantage of the variability in plant growth, actually seems to produce new plants—does produce new plants and apparently has plant culture and plant growth under artificial control. This is simply taking advantage of variability[,] scientific variability [and] inherent variability. So[54] although we cannot actually influence social instincts, by taking advantage of the variations in these instincts, we can actually train them in one direction or another. And I fancy, [even though] most of[55] this social cultivation has been, perhaps, in the unfavorable direction, there is just as much possibility of favorable cultivation according to that variability[. Race][56] issues and feelings, although individually and collectively [variable,] connect themselves with these phenomena. Variability[,] therefore[,] provides a margin of social control and establishes, it seems to me, the moral responsibility of society in these matters.

Now that would seem to be contrary to an important fact, a fact to which I wish to call your attention. Race antipathy is instinctive (it is a matter of instinct [and] it is a matter of individual instinct) which would seem to be contrary to the position that we have taken that as a matter of fact, society can control it, and individuals can control it. It must not be argued[, however, that] because it is instinctive in appeal and operation that it is spontaneous. It is not: it is cultivated, very often deliberately cultivated, and much is not only cultivated but[57] controlled and modified. It can be controlled and modified, and [when] left to itself, it subsides. As a matter of fact[,] you will find comparatively little race antipathy under a system of slavery. The [overwhelming] dominance of a certain class [means that it] does not feel jeopardized[,] and because it does not feel jeopardized, the instinctive antipathy lapses. Consequently[,] when you find an era of actual antipathy, or what we call "prejudice," you are apt to confront not a static era or period in human society, but a period of change.

The second, the subtler, and the more frequently [noted phase of] race antagonism *only* develops[58] with emancipation and subsequent rivalries by which the status of one group is apt to be invaded [or challenged by] the status of another group. There is violent intensification whenever race contacts pass from one stage or level to another, especially when they pass from an automatic to a voluntary basis—as they do, for example, when a slave system is abolished, or[59] when the society takes on quite a different function, as, for example, the state of one society at peace and the state of the same society at war. Consider that the activities of a society at war are automatic and not so voluntary as the activities of the same society at peace[,] and you will see, for example, why a race group that is unpopular in a state of peace suddenly becomes popular and fuses into [the military mainstream] when the war breaks out. When the group is needed, class differences are forgotten [and antagonistic groups] unite to face the enemy [because unity is in their] common interest. Any interest[,] therefore[,] can span [and] bridge racial and class differences and antagonisms, [and often does.][60]

I want to call your attention[61] in this lecture to a matter, to a [paradoxical] difference, which has not yet been explained, between the race sense of [some] groups and the race sense of other groups. In the main[,] the racial feeling of the French and of the native Englishman (I mean the Englishman at home) is of a type which decreases as the unlike race or group approaches the civilization type. In other words, he likes *you* more and [associates] with *you* more, the nearer *you* approach to his civilization type. Whereas the Colonial British (those English in the colonies) [along with] the Australian and the American, as a rule, seem to be of the opposite type[:][62] they are more violently repelled by you the nearer you approach to their civilization type. Now that is a very paradoxical and a very definite phenomenon that has scarcely been noticed, and because it has scarcely been noticed, it is as yet unexplained.

A certain western professor,[63] Dr. R[obert] E. Park,[64] with whom it was my advantage to come into contact, suggests that a distinction of his between primary and secondary groups accounts for this paradox. He believes,[65] for example, that [what] he calls a primary group [is] a group which is essentially a social unit, and a secondary group [is] a group that has been transplanted and is in process of absorbing other groups. He would call the United States a secondary group,[66] for example, because of the rapid distribution of wealth and the rapid development of class, and so on. He would say that the society[67] [that is rapidly expanding, functions] with reactions that are the exact opposite of a primary group or what he would call a primitive society. [Or to reverse the order,][68] an old-established society would characterize the former type and a new society the latter type. In [that] case, he would say that in the former or primary type of society[,] the nearer you approach the type, the more recognition you get, and the racial feeling and class feeling there decrease proportionally—and in the [latter type, the expanding society,][69] it would be the opposite.

Now, the final thing I wish to call to your attention is that color or other cardinal race differences are not the seat of these differences at all. They complicate, but they do not cause these issues. It is enlightening and necessary for us to turn our attention to quarters of the world that actually prove this. The racial problems and the class issues of European states, particularly those in [s]outhern Europe and the Balkans, actually prove that color or other cardinal race differences do not cause such issues, because every social issue and discrimination which prevails under a feeling between race groups prevails there simply between groups, [which,][70] although they may be ethnically different, do not belong to cardinally different races.

It is really a problem of social [conformity.][71] Whenever one group is assimilating the culture of another group[, there is often an acute reaction. Unfortunately, we do not have an] opportunity in the course [of these lectures] to study at close range the Lithuanian question[.][72] [The Lithuanians are a peculiarly] assimilative people [like] the Polish Jew. The race prejudice against the Lithuanian indicates that whenever you have a group that is in the process of rapidly assimilating the culture of another group, you will have this outcropping of violent class or racial feeling.

And yet in proportion [as a] color [or] a cardinal race difference does enter into these issues[, the feelings] become violent [and] much more inveterate than a minor instinct.[73] [What distinguish][74] race issues [from class issues] is that [the former][75] seem different[, even though both arise in the practical struggle to attain] a common social good. Paradoxical[ly] enough,[76] any groups that are living in a common [society,] even though they have different functions [and] different relations, must have a common social end in the main. [Race groups, like class groups, compete for the same social good. But] these [race struggles and race] issues generate a perfect vortex of ⟨⟨more fundamental antagonisms⟩⟩ that are very often regarded as so ⟨⟨ultimate⟩⟩ and beyond solution [that they seem] distinct from class questions[; but] they are common, differing only in degree. They are very violent, I grant you, but the very fact that they sometimes break into class issues proves that they are only a very virulent kind of class question, after all.

Race feelings [have] ⟨⟨an undetermined relation to population⟩⟩[. These feelings become] intensified [with][77] marked variations ⟨⟨in relative proportions⟩⟩ [of population,] largely, I fancy, because groups become conscious of themselves whenever there is change[.][78] Where conditions are suitable[,] the sense of the group prevails. The same number of people engaged in an activity which can separate them out in the public mind, will generate a race issue very much more violent than the race issue generated by the same number of people who cannot be thought of *en masse*. So that if you [had][79] in a city population a race or a class that was exclusively engaged in certain pursuits (as, for example, the factory class) the same number of people would generate a class or a race feeling many times more violent than that of the same number of people in different pursuits. The economic [situation that causes them][80] to be thought of in the mass aggravates the situation.

Of course, as I shall call to your attention in the next lecture,[81] color is one of these peculiar social characteristics that promotes [the] reaction of group sense and therefore is one of the important factors in this kind of a group feeling. [Eradication of] economic [and political] disability seems to require legislative change, legislative control. Whenever we have this [violation of the creed of] political equality[, the social mind] seems either to blot out differences [or to force us to] tolerate discrepancies [between our professed ideals and our social practices,] as we are tolerating them in this country. The Fourteenth and Fifteenth Amendments[,] having been adopted before they were possible in point of [fact, have] necessarily lapsed until practical conditions could catch up with them. It seems that under democratic conditions[,] because legal right or political participation has been formally granted[,] institutions [are] always [distorted][82] further than would happen under other conditions.

Whenever social prejudice prevails[,] you have race relations in a secondary stage. Social[83] prejudice is indicative of an achievement of a certain advanced grade in the contact of the groups. The contact of the groups at this stage is very often complicated by the fact of blood intermixture. Blood intermixture starts as [the heritage of] slavery, concubinage, or worse. [At first,] social inequality between the groups [means] that [the] mixed blood is the only class to be recognized by the dominant class and the first group to take [advantage of] their adoption, education, and [exposure to the] civilization of the prevailing or dominant group. And yet as things progress[,] there is a very universal and a very violent reaction against the mixed blood. The first reaction on the part of the dominant group seems to repudiate its own action and seeks to stem the current of events.

[A secondary] reaction that perhaps we are just in sight of [in this country is] the increasing sense of retaliat[ory] race pride and integrity which is developed in the other group as soon as it comes under the pressure of social discrimination. These social discriminations and problems are to be considered in the next lecture. They are only remotely touched by legislation.[84] There are some which really seem to me after all, the final stage [in] race relations and problems[,] and indicate that the race questions and issues have passed into the final stage.

In dealing with class issues[,] certain students of society[,] as well as certain practical reformers[,] are often compell[ed] to think that the acute phases are the phases indicating the final step of solution, and they rather welcome acute phases because they regard them in that light. I fancy that we shall have to come [to a] position in race problems [analysis where we][85] regard some of the reactions of our present situation in America as indicative of a final stage, and welcome them as such, because they seem to be born of the very last effort of society to stem the inevitable when they confront [the reality of progressive change.] But, of course[,] they can only have that sense of jeopardy when they are confronted by an apparent and what may be an actual realization that the fetish of the distinctions is about the only thing that is left.

NOTES: LECTURE 3

1. Clause deleted following "are": "because no matter how far back the practices of race may go".

2. Word order changed. Original: "what we shall endeavor to turn our attention to now in this lecture will be those conditions which are—even though they may be centuries old—working today."

3. "can" replaces original "cannot".

4. Word deleted following "meaning": "by".

5. Paragraph break at beginning of sentence ignored.

6. Bibliography was not attached to lecture transcriptions. Locke may have been referring to the bibliography that accompanied the syllabus to the course that he had privately printed. Those works were:

Bryce, Lord James. *Studies in History and Jurisprudence*. London: Oxford University Press, 1901.

Stephenson, Gilbert T. *Race Distinctions in American Law*. New York and London: Appleton & Co., 1910.

Zollschan, Ignaz. *Das Rassenprobleme*. Vienna & Leipzig: W. Braumuller, 1912.

Lapouge, Georges Vacher. *Les Selections sociales*. Paris: A. Fontemoing, 189[6].

Tarde, Gabriel. *The Laws of Imitation*. New York: Holt, 1903, pp. 213–43, 310–22.

Mecklin, John Moffatt. *Democracy and Race Friction*. New York: Macmillan Co., 1914. Chaps. I and V,1–18, 357–81.

American Journal of Sociology, 1914–1915.
    a. Vol. 20, no.4 "Schmoller on Class Conflicts."
    b. Vol. 19, Park, Robert E. "Racial Assimilation in Secondary Groups."

Stone, Alfred H. *Studies in the American Race Problem*. New York: Doubleday, Page & Co., 1908.

Murphy, Edgar Gardner. *The Basis of Ascendancy*. New York: Longmans, Green, and Co., 1909.

7. Fragmentary sentence deleted following "attitude": "If the evidence [...] are scientific, then we may be warranted in [...] that we shall [...] our initial observation of the facts, our whole procedure is open to serious objection."

8. "with" replaces original "and".

9. Word deleted from beginning of sentence: "and".

10. Irretrievable fragment deleted from beginning of paragraph: "Here we have a really [...] sociological and historical [....]"

11. "although" replaces "and".

12. "phrase" replaces "word".

13. Most likely that friend was Dr. Horace Kallen (1882–1974), a philosopher, cultural pluralist, and Harvard College friend of Alain Locke. Kallen was an instructor at the University of Wisconsin from 1911 to 1918.

14. Word deleted following "university": "in".

15. Phrase deleted following "according to": "the characteristics [...] upon".

16. I have been unable to identify Professor Cobb. Several potential Cobbs have been ruled out. Dr. James Adlair Cobb, a lecturer on commercial paper, did not begin teaching at Howard University until fall 1916, after Locke's lectures. He is also not known to have written on sociology. Dr. William Montague Cobb, (1904–1990), the Howard University professor and physician, did write on physical anthropology, but he was too young. An obscure sociologist, John Chandler Cobb, (1858–1933) did produce a book on scientific methods to sociology, but the book appeared in 1934, and he was never a professor. Locke might have had in mind the Georgian, Thomas R. R. Cobb, who wrote extensively on slavery. But more likely, Professor Cobb was probably someone Locke had discovered in England or in Germany. The concept of the "consciousness of kind," which Locke refers to in the same paragraph, derives from Franklin Giddings (1855–1931). (*Howard University Catalogue* vol. 10 (May 1916) and vol. 11 (May 1917); William Montague Cobb, *Human Materials in American Institutions Available for Anthropological Study?* (Philadelphia: The Wistar Institute of Anatomy and Biology, 1933); John Chandler Cobb, *The Application of Scientific Methods to Sociology* (Boston: Chapman & Grimes, 1934); Thomas R. R. Cobb, *Law of Negro Slavery in the United States of America* (New York: Negro Universities Press, 1968; orig. pub. 1858); Franklin Giddings, *The Principles of Sociology* (New York: Johnson Reprint Corp., 1970; orig. pub. 1926),*passim*).

17. Word deleted following "So": "that".

18. "as" replaces original "them was not".

19. "having" replaces original "they have".

20. Paragraph break inserted at beginning of sentence.

21. "in" replaces original "with".

22. "as" replaces original "than grow up".

23. "that is" replaces original "as".

24. "counter" replaces original "contradictory".

25. Word order changed. Original: "the civilized human being has ingrained in his disposition as a civilized man by centuries of heritage these distinctions."

26. Words deleted following "disposition": "as a civilized man".

27. Word order changed. Original: "are rather caused by legislation".

28. "being" replaces original "are".

29. "the difference" replaces original "itself".

30. The phrase "stereotyping function of the law" was written in the margin in Locke's hand. Locke may have added these words to the text in the 1920s, since our

common notion of a stereotype as a simplified attitude or group image, was popularized by Walter Lippmann in his *Public Opinion* (New York: Harcourt, Brace and Co., 1922). But given that Locke uses the construction "stereotyping" to describe how the law fixes an attitude in our minds, it is possible he may have adopted the term from the English legal usage that preceded Lippmann's publication. See John Morley's *The Life of William Ewart Gladstone*, vol. 3 1880–1898 (London: Macmillan and Co., Ltd., 1903), 331, where he states "There ought to be no stereotyping of our minds against modifications."

31. Word deleted from beginning of sentence: "Where".

32. Written in the margin in Locke's handwriting.

33. Phrase deleted following "serf [....]": "as well as to extent the basis of the".

34. Words deleted following "grouping": "more or less".

35. "Because" deleted from the beginning of the sentence.

36. "especially among" replaces original "in".

37. Word order changed. Original: "quickly [...] conditions to adjust themselves [...] race differences and differences of physical type."

38. Word deleted following "helotage": "existing".

39. "are" replaces "is".

40. Word order changed. Original: "not so treated".

41. Word deleted from beginning of sentence: "and".

42. The term *kraal* has two meanings in Afrikaans—as a "cattle byre," a thorn bush or earthen enclosure often used by farmers at the Cape to house stock, and as a human settlement, specifically a circle of huts in which the "Khoi-khoin" people lived in South Africa—neither of which conforms precisely to Locke's use of the term here, that is, as a form of residential segregation that guaranteed access to black labor. See E. W. H. Lategan, *The Hottentots (Khoi-Khoin)* (Capetown and Johannesburg: Perskor Pub., 1981), 16–17. In the early twentieth century, "location" was the term used by South Africans to describe the area outside cities where black workers were forced by custom to live. It was the location which functions as Locke suggests here, as a segregated area next to the town which guaranteed white access to black labor. See Basil Davidson, *Report on Southern Africa* (London: Jonathan Cape, 1952), 83–91. In 1948 the term "location" began to be replaced by the word "township" or "Bantu township," which reflected the transformation of segregation into apartheid. With the rise to power of the Nationalist Party in 1948 and the subsequent passage of the Group Areas Act of 1950 and the Native Resettlement Act of 1954, it became illegal in South Africa for blacks to live outside the township in urban areas. See Paul Maylam, *A History of the African People of South Africa: From the Early Iron Age to the 1970s* (New York: St. Martin's Press, 1986), 178–81. Also valuable is John Rex, "The Compound, the Reserve and the Location: Three Essential Institutions of South African Labour Exploitation," *The South African Labour Bulletin* vol. 1, no. 4 (1971). Locke may have gained this particular use of the word kraal from his Oxford friend, Pixley Ka Isaka Seme (1881?–1951), a black South African and a founding member of the African Native Congress. Jeffrey Butler notes that kraal is often used as a verb: "I have heard Afrikaners say 'We are going to kraal these Blacks off into a location.'" (Telephone interview, 10 February 1990, and correspondence, 22 August 1990, with Jeffrey Butler)

43. For a discussion of the legalized Jewish ghetto in Europe, see Louis Wirth, *The Ghetto* (Chicago: The University of Chicago Press, 1956; orig. pub. 1928), 48–53, 124–30. Wirth suggests a slightly different set of causes for the emergence of the Jewish ghetto. "The ghetto arose, in the first instance, out of a body of practices and needs of the Jewish population. Gradually it became an established institution without the Jews themselves being aware of the invisible walls that they were building around their community. Only when it became formally recognized and sanctioned by law, or, rather, decreed by law, however, did it become an object of resentment because is [*sic*] was a symbol of subjuga-

tion," (50–51). Still, Locke would argue that the economic viability of the Jewish population was central to European society's willingness to transform Jewish self-segregation into
so rigid a legal institution. As Wirth notes in his discussion of Frankfort, "The Jews, with
their partial monopoly of trade and finance, were the very core of the commercial and
industrial life of that city," (51).

44. Word deleted and word order changed following "organic." Original: "very often
it is not".

45. "and yet are nevertheless forced to live under restricted status, then" replaces
"so".

46. Paragraph break inserted at beginning of sentence.

47. "The modern social mind" replaces original "they".

48. "and" replaces "but".

49. "that are operative even in the absence of legal restrictions. Such social facts"
replaces original "[....] but they".

50. Locke may be referring to such states as New York, which did not free all its slaves
until 5 July 1827, and Pennsylvania, which did not free all its slaves until 1808. See A. Leon
Higginbotham, Jr., *In the Matter of Color: Race and the American Legal Process: The Colonial
Period* (London: Oxford University Press, 1978), 143–50, 304–5.

51. "To" replaces original "from".

52. Word deleted following "problem": "that".

53. Paragraph break inserted at beginning of sentence.

54. Words deleted following "So": "that perhaps".

55. Words deleted following "of": "the if".

56. "Race" replaces original "and the".

57. Sentence broken up and word order changed after "but". Original: "it can be
controlled and modified—it is controlled and modified, and left to itself it subsides."

58. Irretrievable fragment deleted following "develops": "[...] then with a [...] change
in human society or an impending change [...] in the group relationships. It only
develops".

59. Words deleted following "or": "when they do perhaps".

60. "and often does" replaces original "which, as a matter of fact ... it is an invariable
accompaniment of such a state of affairs."

61. Word order changed following "attention": "to a matter, in this lecture".

62. Word deleted following "type": "that".

63. Word order changed. Original: "A certain western professor, with whom it was my
advantage to come into contact, Dr. R. E. Park,".

64. Locke may have discussed these ideas with Dr. Robert E. Park (1864–1944) at the
Universal Races Congress in London in 1911, or at Booker T. Washington's Tuskegee
Institute in 1912. Park's "Racial Assimilation in Secondary Groups with Particular Reference to the Negro," which appeared in the *American Journal of Sociology* 19 (March
1914):606–23 and in the *Publications of the American Sociological Society* 8 (July 1914):66–83
does not specifically address the phenomena Locke discusses here; it does outline Park's
theory that nationalist sentiment among African Americans is a logical outcome of
blocked access and assimilation into mainstream American life.

65. Word order changed. Original: "believes that, for example".

66. Word order changed. Original: "group because, for example, of the".

67. Word order changed. Original: "society [...] as a society that must [...] reactions
that are the exact opposite of [...] or what he would call a primitive society."

68. "Or to reverse the order" replaces original "So that".

69. "latter type, the expanding society," replaces original "other".

70. "which" replaces original "that are".

71. "conformity" replaces original "[...] thus to take a group [...]".

72. "[...] by Austria" deleted after "question".

73. Irretrievable fragment deleted following "minor instinct": "race antagonisms [....] class antagonisms, that the actual social influence of the group is said [...] to differ, although of course since they live in common society, if the society has any common end at all, they must proportionately share in that common end."

74. "What distinguish" replaces original "the differientation then of".

75. "the former" replaces original "it".

76. Word deleted following "enough": "because".

77. "with" replaces original "in".

78. Word deleted following "change": "and".

79. "had" replaces original "would".

80. "situation that causes them" replaces original "[...] they are likely".

81. Words deleted following "lecture": "the [...] not stigma [...]".

82. "distorted" replaces original "[...] to their".

83. Words deleted from beginning of sentence: "So that".

84. Paragraph break at beginning of sentence ignored.

85. "analysis where we" replaces original "[...] to".

4

Modern
Race Creeds
and Their Fallacies

WE HAVE GOTTEN to a critical point in the discussion of this subject, a point where we must really scrutinize our motives because, if you recall, we pledged ourselves to a perfectly dispassionate and scientific examination of the subject. Here we reach a point where we have to deal with what is really irrational and something which we shall have to, in the end, condemn. And yet if we do it out of hand (which would be tantamount to doing it out of court) we ourselves would be subject to the same kind of criticisms that we level at our opponents. We [pursued][1] a disinterested account of the situation just as far as that was possible, and that disinterested account ends practically with the third lecture. Here, now, we must try, rather constructively, to survey the contemporary problems and situations in matters of race and to see if we cannot really get some sort of bearing, which, of course, must aim undoubtedly both to explain and to condemn the false practices of race that are so prevalent.

We shall not condemn them except in terms of a scientific explanation of them. I myself am quite convinced that a scientific explanation of them is sufficient condemnation. It is sufficient within the boundaries of the kind of undertaking that we have in hand.

We are dealing now not so much with practices as with the creeds that lie [in] back of certain practices. We must distinguish all through, I fancy, between the creed which motivates the practice and the social practice itself. The [emergence] of creed in race is one of the most difficult elements. It has not always been connected with the practice of race. Although there can be no very definite decision, I fancy that the older practices of race were different from our modern practices on this very point—that they weren't reinforced by a doctrine of race at all[.]² They were therefore merely instinctive practices and not the rather iniquitous kind of reinforcement of irrational positions³ that we confront when we confront anything like a modern race creed. The race creed, therefore, is essentially a rather modern thing, and an account of this important factor seems necessary if we want to get any group opinion of [the] contemporary situations [of] race contacts. At present these race creeds seem to be forces that one must take into consideration, because, as you can see, even when they do not originate practices[,] they reinforce them to the extent that they are, so to speak, an entrenchment for the kind of condition which we discussed in the preceding lecture.

Lord Cromer, in what is a feature in his very illuminating book⁴ *Ancient and Modern Imperialism* [,] gives in an appendix a conjecture which I take to be more important than the bulk of his work.⁵ In this appendix he suggests a distinction between ancient and modern society on the ground of what [he] names race creed, or the psychological complication in differences of race, in creeds of race[.] He distinguishes therefore between the mere instinctive practices and the indoctrinated kind of practices, which we confront all over the world today. If this is true[,] [then] color prejudice and race prejudice are by no means identical. Race prejudice, in the objective sense, is something which in the preceding lecture we have traced to the very root of history.

But color prejudice is a strange sort of aberration which seems peculiar to the modern mind.⁶ Lord Cromer is, I think, very right in believing that this is a distinctively modern feature. Color prejudice, then, he regards as a phenomenon in modern society. He says, "I am not aware that any competent scholar has ever examined into the question //of the stage// of the history⁷ //of [the] world at which difference of colour, as distinguished from difference of race, acquired the importance which it certainly now possesses// [as] a social and political factor."⁸ After stating that[, he notes that] the best authorities are of the opinion that there was no definite indication of color [prejudice] in the ancient world. The habit of thought of modern and ancient people may in some degree be explained on the ground that the former enslaved only the colored races[,] while the ancients doomed all whom they conquered to slavery.

The first conflict [involving] differences based on color is of comparatively recent growth. It seems probable that it received great stimulus from the discoveries of the fifteenth and sixteenth centuries[, combined with] the rise of the African slave trade and [the] era of commercial expansion and exploitation.

Of course, slavery and actual color differences cannot be the real causes for racial antipathies any more than political subjection is the only source of the sense of superiority which we see[9] possess[ed] by certain dominant peoples. And yet it is very significant, I think, that contemporaneous with the enormous expansion of horizon that was attendant upon fifteenth[-]and sixteenth[-]century world voyaging and discovery[,] there seems to have come into the world this kind of social and mental epidemic which has been running a rather virulent course ever since. The history, the pathological history, of society will undoubtedly have to cope with this and really trace it, perhaps, to its cause. At any rate, as far as we are concerned, the historical antecedents of race prejudice—and we use the term meaning color prejudice—against the darker races by the races attributing to themselves Aryan or Caucasian descent cannot be traced back any further than this period.

Ever since then there has been a sort of insecurity in which men have had to rather entrench themselves in their social positions[.] By that I mean that just as soon as the modern commercial era dawned, society has ever since been in a more fluid state and by virtue of that[,] any class position could not be as secure as it was under a noncompetitive, noncommercial regime. It was [necessary to be] rather conscious of class lines due to the rather extraordinary difficulty of maintaining [social position] in a society of that type. So that really[,] snobbishness and [the compulsion for] class monopoly seem to have sprung up along with this plant of color antipathy.

Regarding the historical and the social factors of color prejudice as of some importance, I think we should not overlook the fact that, after all, the psychological factors are the [controlling] ones. These factors are as yet undetermined, and yet their study should be one of the most important aspects of social sciences, for the very good reason that they offer to take us to the very heart of the social instincts and to show us what it is, really, that generates what we call the social mind. The study of society in terms of its psychological factors has, of course, been attempted[;] and yet this single clue which promises some [real advancement] toward comprehension of the nature of the social mind has been ominously neglected by the sociologists. I fancy their neglect has been somewhat deliberate because the very irrationality of certain social modes and creeds undoubtedly is to be revealed by the study of this factor.

No one should minimize the fact that race antipathy involves some instincts as well as some practices in human society that are in themselves normal and healthy, and perhaps never to be eradicated. Yet it is not [*necessary*] to think that because of them[, the related but][10] abnormal manifestations of race prejudice are to be condoned or tolerated. [M]odern[11] science has it that a thing is healthful or abnormal[12] not so much according to its essence as according to its effect—not so much according to its nature in itself as to what it brings about, what it causes[.] And surely if these healthy, normal social instincts run the wrong way, they can be condemned, and, if we treat them remedially, can be [controlled] without eradicating them altogether. Because to think of eradicating[13] from human society the social instincts upon which racial prejudice is based would be something like the heroic surgery that would treat a cancer [by] extracting [an organ.] The very reaction, or the nature of the very reaction, of race prejudice shows how vital an instinct it is rooted upon. It is perhaps the most inhibitive of all of the social instincts. It is the thing which pulls a man in his social activities more than, perhaps, any other single plea. It is the thing which seems to go beyond his reason and to lay grip upon him in such a way that he may [not be able to rise above its][14] influence.

Consciousness of kind [becomes a problem when] working in an abnormal way. It is a force[15] which the society [finds to be][16] absolutely [necessary, and yet in excess, leads] to the maintenance of unhealthy and rather unjust distinctions in human society. We have therefore to deal with something which, though we must regard it as the blight of modern society, [is] something which nevertheless can only be eradicated through its being transformed [in]to a healthy, normal, and rational expression.

One of the earliest attempts to study social instincts unfortunately came long before the development of modern sociological methods. It was Bacon's remarkable anticipation of this phase in his famous study of the idols.[17] The Baconian "idol" is, after all, just this kind of a social instinct, of which racial antipathy is one of the most potent. There has been as yet nothing, perhaps, more profound than the incisive remarks of Bacon with regard to the nature and the derivation of the idols of human society.

I tried to compare race prejudice as disinterestedly as I could with the four types of idols that Bacon distinguishes, and in spite of the fact that I made all due allowance for the very arbitrary and artificial aspect of Bacon's classification, it seemed that really race antipathy could not be identified with any one of the four groups[.]¹⁸ The [way that] indoctrination into this [social instinct] has been [a] deliberate transmission from one person to another makes it resemble more of what he calls an "idola theatri" than anything else.¹⁹

[Race antipathy]²⁰ has in its very nature all of the irrational elements which Bacon described as characteristic of the social idols[.] But, at least as we confront it today, it is a constant indoctrination of race by which a single person may become a center for the spread of a very vicious and very irrational but nevertheless very [effective] kind of influence[.] [It will]²¹ appeal to some of the most fundamental of human instincts and band men together in an actual [orgy] of discrimination on the basis of projected and unexamined distinction[s] between them and another group. We see this sort of thing working not only over the commercial line but working within the very broad race distinctions which in themselves are supposed to possess a certain kind of homogenous social character. By that I mean to say that the same kind of instinct can prevail within Caucasian groups. It is not to be differentiated, for example, from the racial hatred which has become [widespread] in Europe at the present time.

Now, for example, in the Rhine District the French and the Germans have [become extremely conscious of distinctions between them,] so that there is no Frenchman and no German [intermixture] ethnically in that district. In that district there had always been maintained a certain kind of racial merger [such that a] person was not quite German and not quite Gallic[.]²² [I]n spite of that fact, there have been repeated outcroppings, in that district, of the same kind of racial antipathies within the group and directed at times toward those [people] ethnically [of mixed nationalities that are] expresse[d]²³ in the antipathy between the Caucasian and the darker races. This has been periodic—it has not been continuously maintained. But a certain class has been interested in its deliberate maintenance[, interested] that the system of that racial hatred should not die out even after the growth of it has died down[.]

We have today, in the Alsace-Lorraine question, a deliberate outcropping of that same kind of [group antipathy caused by external] influence that²⁴ [in its] most virulent form cannot be more virulent than the question of racial [conflict,] proving it seems, our view [that][25] indoctrination can operate to such an extent that over certain issues racial antipathies can actually spring up between divergent sects or divisions of the same race or the same ethnic strain.[26]

Of course, that feature which makes this racial antipathy so much of a problem in the relations of Caucasian and non-Caucasian peoples is the fact that color is an artificial and rather overemphasized stigma, [and] is alone sufficient to arouse the reaction[;] whereas with other stigmata that are not so obvious the reactions are apt to lie dormant until they are artificially aroused by some shibboleth of social issues, like [when], for example, a man through an admission about himself might betray the group to which he belongs.

I was extremely interested [to learn], for example, in taking a trip I had the good fortune to take, as far east as the Brown Provinces[27] of Austria [that] a number of people come within the range of the same kind of racial antipathy [characteristic] of Caucasian stock[:] some [are the] Slavic, [especially the] Lithuanians. One of the Lithuanians, particularly, told me [that] language or accent was practically as [*operative*] as color is with us, and that if they could disguise their tongue they could get up in society very well[.] But if they betrayed [their nationality] by their language in society[,] in public places like restaurants and theaters, they were immediately subjected to the most humiliating kind of treatment, showing after all [that][28] any arbitrary, artificial factor can control the situation [even though][29] color by its very obviousness makes the [reaction] more virulent than perhaps any other single factor. Those, therefore, who are subject to a color discrimination are simply the easy victims of a force in human society which operates along lines of other factors wherever there is this conscious indoctrination of race.

Now, as to how this conscious indoctrination of race came up is another of the mysteries into which I can only, perhaps, take a glimpse, and here, too, with a conjecture. But it seems to me that this kind of race sense is a by-product of certain stages of human growth and development, just like some virulent toxin[, it is like] a poison that is a by-product, for example, of a healthy process of assimilation in the human body. The way in which society infects itself in certain stages with these elements and creeds would rather prove that[.] Because I do not think any society would consciously make itself the victim of some of the rather extraordinary conditions that persisting in a race creed will bring upon it. It is really [a] social plague and becomes so after a few generations of indulgence in it. So I do not think any society would deliberately [bring upon itself] all these evils. For example, if the South had realized the kind of contradiction in which it would place itself, it would recant possibly (at least the sensible people would have recanted) from the race creed with which it was [saddled for so long.][30]

A study of European society is particularly useful in this respect because we want to get a fair comparative basis for whatever may work [to understand] the class at hand. The spread of anti-Semitism, which has been very closely studied by a few Jewish savants[,] is directly analogous to the question of race antipathy which we see in this country. Anti-Semitism, [as a practice is not new: in] Europe, [the Jew] has had several periods of persecution[;] but anti-Semitism is particularly a modern creed[,] and it seems to have originated almost simultaneously in France and in Russia[,] and to have spread from both those centers until now it affects most of the bureaucratic classes of European governments[.]

[Anti-Semitism] seems to be a creed of the bureaucratic and aristocratic classes [handed down] to be taken up by the bourgeoisie [in modern] society, where, as a matter of fact, actual contact with the Jew is for economic reasons very necessary.[31] So the bureaucratic classes have foisted the creed upon the middle classes which have no need for it. Anti-Semitism[, which has flourished] within the last thirty or thirty-five years, is something which shows that from certain centers [a] very virulent kind of race creed can spread. Anti-Semitism [first] appeared in militaristic circles largely, particularly in France, where it culminated in the[32] Dreyfus affair, a matter of military prejudice.[33] In Russia it was undoubtedly a matter of prejudice in educational circles, be it said to their shame, but from its narrow [origin,] it has so spread until certain political and governmental issues in Europe today are so complicated by the factor of Anti-Semitism that Anti-Semitism is sometimes more important than the issues which bring it about[;] and cabinets rise and fall on the issue.

The second crop of race prejudice which we encounter in this country is simpl[y an analogy to the type of virulent Anti-Semitism we see in Europe. The flowering of prejudice against Negroes][34] is a plant the seeds of which were sown during the days of Reconstruction. We are probably in the midst of the hardest of it, let us say, today, let us say tonight, particularly.[35]

A scientific study of race prejudice awaits the further development of social psychology and, I fancy, that this social psychology will show a certain analogy between race issues and class issues. The closest analogies between class problems and race problems involve a sentimental issue. Race issues are only very virulent forms of class issues, because as they can be broken up into class issues they become possible of solution in society. Recent observers have attempted this [study of race issues from a class standpoint] and have not gone far, because in this day of social reform[, studies of race problems] are in the hands of people who belong to one school or another. In other words[,] it is very hard to be impartial.

The most competent social psychologists and economists [are] in Germany [and are members of a] school [of thought] that could very well deal with this issue. [But that school] is hopelessly split and cannot be impartial. I happen to know two of the men who, if they could combine, would be competent perhaps to work not only [on race, but also on a study] of classes in society[.] But one of them, Professor Schmoller,[36] a full professor at the University of Berlin[, is a member of the] bureacratic [establishment]; the other [is] a Jewish professor[37] who because of race, though an assistant professor, can never hope to become a full professor.[38] Therefore[,] you see that prejudice within the university [divides] the two men who as scholars really should confront the same scientific problems [but are prevented from doing so] by an [adherence to social] custom; and [the most][39] these men can do consistent with their [positions] is to admit the irrational element in color prejudice. They just leave the matter there not caring to trust [each other enough to collaborate and] being thus in doubt as to whether or not reason can ever be [successful] as a cure for what is irrational in practice. That still remains to be seen. Perhaps we should be satisfied [to observe that such][40] antipathies originate in [the feelings groups have for other] groups[;] [the][41] spread [of such antipathies] to new communities [is not] by accident [and will continue to occur unless][42] there [is][43] some way in which the controlling external conditions can be checked. At any rate, until these can be explained, race prejudice will remain something of an enigma. It seems to be peculiarly enigmatical, because it is prevalent in the very kind of society that professes to be free from it, namely, a democratic society[. Such societies] are more often the prey of such feelings than monarchical societies. That is true of class issues and doubly true of race issues. There is, for example, more actual snobbery, class snobbery, in America than you can find in an autocracy in Europe, because there seems to be, at least in the minds of the people, a need for arbitrary [class distinctions] where class lines are relatively unstable[. In a democracy, the social superiority of elites is] something which the forms of society do not guarantee to them except as they earn it[.] Consequently[,] you see class feeling going to greater extremes in the more fluid kinds of society where class distinctions are more easily passed over.

In some correspondence with a friend of mine, now at the University of Wisconsin, I had an opportunity to discuss with him the relative strength of denominational feeling and race feeling.[44] Being a Jew, he had certain information that I never could get—information from the side of the Jew as to their attitude towards mixed marriages[,][45] as in Anglican Jewry where a mixed marriage does not seem incompatible with orthodoxy[.] But he pointed out very clearly to me that Jewish intermarriage was never possible where the Jewish faith was maintained in orthodox form, arguing that religious denominationalism was stronger than race feeling unsupported by denominational feeling[.] Because in Anglican Jewry there was very little objection on the part of the Jew as contrasted with a strong objection wherever the Jewish faith was orthodox. It does seem then that where social solidarity is maintained and established both class issues and race issues are [as intense] as they are in democratic societies or in societies where social solidarity has to be deliberately maintained. Wherever society, therefore, is [stable and secure,] we find a relative shading off of these issues. The growth of unity in Prussia illustrates this because Prussia was not anti-Semitic until through universal training the Jew became a very serious rival in bureaucratic positions and military [appointments.] An artificial handicap had to be put on him in the minds of the dominant class to prevent him from cutting away their monopoly.

Now[46] race prejudice, in so far as we are scientifically able [to determine it, is rooted in a] psychologically false standard of social judgment. [But] I want at this point to insist upon what seems to me to be [something that is] very basic[:] if you confront race prejudice as it is, in other words, if you argue with it or fight with it upon its own plane, you have acknowledged it. Some of the most forceful arguments against race prejudice are guilty of the same fallacies [of arguing upon the same false] basis of judgment of which race prejudice is its expression.

A[47] man wholly innocent, fortunately, of [these] matters, [and] dealing merely with practical contracts of the world of letters and art, said very distinctly that to attempt to qualify in a certain race way in art and

letters was practically an admission of a double standard of artistic judgment—an admission which he considered to be just as fatal as the assertion against us that we try to controvert. It would fall in line with this
point that there is too much opposition to race prejudice, which simply
confirms it by admitting the standard upon which it is based, and that
in certain relationships the only [sane][48] way is to ignore it and that in
certain aspects it is something which can only be combated through that
attitude which refuses to accept the basis upon which it is pronounced.
This is so different from refusing to accept it in its practical expressions
that I must call attention to it. To contradict race prejudice you must
contradict the basis of judgment. You can contradict and flout the
standard upon which [prejudice][49] is reared and not merely [react to][50]
the mere manifestation of it, because to [react to][51] the mere manifestation of it, is often a concession to it.

Now, the most fundamental fallacy of all is the standard which is
used to justify race superiority. In the last lecture, I traced this standard
as one of the apparently necessary aspects of successful national life. It is
inevitable that peoples who have been successful in political practices
and in social culture should assume certain superiorities and that sense
of superiority passes over into a creed of race superiority. Now this creed
of race superiority must be reckoned with.

The best objective statement of it is that of Professor Ross[, who
lectured] before the American Sociological Society on "What [are] the
Causes of Race Superiority."[52] He traces it to all possible factors and
[analyzes] them all, but seems to feel that the most influential factor is
the simply pragmatic one that it enables a people[53] who believe in it to
be more successful[.][54] In other words, the belief actually strengthens
the inherent [*virtues*] of a people as a social group and leads them to
group action and to a kind of activity which[,] without it[,] they would
never hope to achieve.

If this is so, then Professor Ross agrees with the interpretation which
is given by Ignaz Zollschan, perhaps the most profound scholar of race
issues in the world today, and a Jew who lives in Vienna.[55] He accepts it
at this[,] but says that the crux of the whole matter [is the false identifi-
cation of] race in the biological sense [with] race in the political and
social sense. In other words, he says—which is very simple and yet very
profound—[that] a sense of race superiority is a product of some of the
highest types and phases of civilization. It is often to be regarded as
essential to the life and growth of nations. But when they, from their

race superiority, start to predicate race inferiorities, they confound their standards and pass over to a wholly different basis of judgment. They think that because they have made their type represent what it does that those virtues and qualities are inherent and hereditary[,] and that the accidents and practices of history have been caused by these virtues. They therefore think that it is necessary to be of that race to be a full participant of the civilization type and that really this is a sort of false attribution of cause to what, after all, is merely an effect. So that after they have been as a group socially[,] politically[,] and historically successful, they set out to [affirm] and convince themselves and the world [of their innate superiority.] And the most unfortunate feature of it is the conviction, which amounts to self-deception, that the group is ethnically a unit and has achieved what it has because it is biologically of one stock or blood, whereas all history actually proves that this is false. Some of its success is due to incorporations of other stock.

[Hence, the doctrine of race superiority misrepresents and elevates social and political success] into a biological and ethnological sense [of race] which[,] in fact[,] is not commensurate at all with the practical sense of race which has developed through history. This is a doctrine which is a peculiar blight of the nineteenth[-]century['s] thought and scholarship. The root of it, I am sorry to say, is the root of some of the most fruitful scholarship of the whole era. About the middle of the nineteenth century, a little prior to it really,[56] a great discovery was made in Germany which at the time was invented for the purpose of explaining a new interpretation of history. [In particular,][57] it sprang up in connection with the [language] studies of certain German scholars, particularly [Jakob Ludwig Karl] Grimm,[58] [the collector and writer of folk tales, and the author of the *Grammatik* and the German dictionary.] And it was [Grimm and other German philologists][59] who invented the fiction of the Indo-Germanic peoples and the Indo-Germanic language[. They also translated the notion of the Aryan languages into the notion of] the Aryan peoples—a broad classification of Caucasian groups, which had never been thought of before and which was made necessary by their rather broad outlook upon the world of cosmopolitan culture. In that innocent scholarly derivation, the doctrine of Aryan and Indo-Germanic grouping was born, and since then its degeneration into practical creeds of Aryan and Anglo-Saxon superiority is something which I just simply want to suggest to you because the very suggestion of it is in itself sufficient—particularly since in the second lecture we have traced its derivation as a biological creed. This explains why so much good science has come to the rescue and support of so much bad social theory and bad political practice. It has reinforced theoretically race creeds and biological race theory, and [translated personal biases] into irrational and unjust social practices which have spread over the face of [W]estern civilization and which [are propped] up by the imperialistic systems[,] as we have already explained[. These practices and the need to justify them] have so complicated race contacts and relations that practically there is an imaginary line running around the globe dividing, politically and socially, the darker, or the non-Aryan, from the so-called Aryan peoples. Now, we must study this scientifically[,] or we must [at least] study it rationally. As yet we are not prepared to study it scientifically because sociological science has not reached a point where that is possible. A merely rational survey in a brief treatment of what appear to be the dominant fallacies of this modern creed is what we attempt in the closing section of this lecture.

Now to point out these fallacies is sufficient for our present purpose; as we said, our whole attitude in this consideration is that we have sufficiently condemned when we have explained.

The first is the biological fallacy. It believes practically in race units. It believes, for example, that if the French nation is a nation, there must be a Gallic race. It believes that if Germany is a nation[,] there must be a Teutonic race. It believes [that] if Germany and England should merge[,] there must be a joint race or Anglo-Saxon race [in which both share.] In other words[,] it predicates a physical race for every practical social grouping that it finds necessary. Physical race integrity, however, does not exist within the very groups that seem to predicate so much of their practices upon principles of race. They not only controvert their own notions of race integrity [in practice][60] through miscegenation[,] but [also,] as a matter of fact[,] race purity as such[61] (purity of ethnic strain or blood) is impossible under their conditions of life. It is irretrievable even if it [ever existed and] its maintenance is nothing more than a social fetish, a social fiction. It is manifest that such a social fetish and fiction is unwarranted[.][62] A[63] good deal of the race creed and theory of the present day [is rooted in that] biological fallacy.

There is another fallacy—the fallacy of the masses, ⟨⟨the estimation of peoples in terms of aggregates.⟩⟩ [That fallacy is] something I wish we could be as ingenuous toward as perhaps Plato would have been, or even Bacon, because then we would simply dismiss it with the naive and humorous [*caricature*] deserved by that[64] manifest absurdity of judging people in terms of aggregates, and that should be sufficient to inhibit the practice.

Someone said (I think it was Colton[65]) that half the progress of the inquiry [was seeing that the doctrine of race superiority] was a justification in terms of aggregates which he could prove [was scientifically groundless.] We very often stumble into a morass of a fallacy which is directly against us [when] we justify our progress in terms of aggregates. We had so much property, we had so many churches, we had so much this and so much that [and that is why we were successful]. Now, significant as that is from the point of view of statistics it proves nothing from the point of view of the judgment of group [characteristics] because the essential factor is not the aggregate, but the distribution [of a characteristic in a population] in the first place, and[66] the proportionate rate of increase in the second place. A good deal of our justification[,] which was largely sentimental[,] was conducted in the very terms which are the terms that support the fallacy of the masses. In history, in any sound history, we never judge people in aggregates[:] we judge them in terms of their representative groups and their most representative [people] and often[,] perhaps[,] their most unique achievements. Consequently, for example[, historians will describe] a brilliant group in the age of Pericles [whose achievements] will make [the Greeks the] glory of civilization, without reference, perhaps, to how many [or how few] Greeks were [actually] included within the narrow scope of that social culture.[67] [Historians have constructed a history for Europeans that focuses on outstanding achievements,] which they are able to make typical [of the group] without regard to the aggregate [or the actually small] proportion [of the population] which can be made to represent it.

Now successful peoples never judge themselves in terms of aggregates, but they always insist that unsuccessful peoples should judge themselves in terms of aggregates.[68] Consequently[,] the norm of the group is the norm which is forced upon those who are handicapped. If we constantly used this norm for the judgment of all classes and races, then it would be fair. We are not disputing the norm but merely [its singlehanded][69] application [to] the so-called "inferior" peoples. We point it out as one of the fallacies of race and creed. ⟨⟨The fallacy of the masses [should be avoided and] wherever inevitable, a strict comparison of equivalents must be maintained.⟩⟩

The fallacy of the permanency of race types [is] a race creed that has been discussed and disproved[,] particularly by [Franz] Boas in his book

The Mind of Primitive Man.[70] He shows that [71] race types and class types have a certain [cyclical] element [in] society according to which [they] will rise to a climax and decline according to the necessities of economic reorganization within society[.][72] In consequence[,] the most successful class type or[73] race type must rise to a climax and fall[,] and[74] there is no permanence to be attributed to them[.] ⟨⟨No race or class maintains its social role or relative social position long.⟩⟩ And in fact[,] the more representative they are, the less permanent they are apt to be, which would prove that since all these factors change both under what we know as environmental adaptation and under what we [term][75] modern social growth and development, they are not to be regarded as permanent features [by which] to fasten any set of judgments upon any group of people.

The way, for example, in which under pressure certain classes of Jews and certain classes of the Negro have quickly qualified for a certain standard of living as well as a certain standard of civilization type, [really the social culture of modern America, proves that race types change under environmental adaptation.] But social [*privileges*] [are still bestowed] absolutely [based on][76] the portion of the race or group [that has least] adopt[ed the civilization type. That certain classes have] grown away from [the lower standard of the group aggregate][77] [and are] not representing it *themselves* proves that there isn't any such thing even as permanency of cardinal race types. Any fair examination, for example[,] will prove this assertion and prove that a certain kind of assimilation can work counter to a tradition [of the race] type[.] So that [assimilation][78] will operate independently, and you will find [evidence][79] of a certain blood antecedent having certain cultural antecedents which are different from it, and vice versa.

The fallacy of race ascendancy is the most practical [fallacy] of all. I wish I had time to fully discuss this. The most significant manifestation of it is the feeling in modern society that society ought to be reorganized on a bi-racial system and that a race group should duplicate the social organization within itself and keep to itself, maintaining its solidarity [with the rest of society] only [through the] merest sort of economic cooperation which seems necessary for the [functioning] of society. Now this code is the code of practical modern statesmanship. I say that, realizing that we are acquainted with it as it has been practiced, for example, by the advocates of white supremacy in this country. They have said: "Let the Negro develop within and form a separate and distinct society. Let society be reorganized by races and give him every-thing which is necessary for such reorganization[.]'' [The dominant race has] stimulated and encouraged [this notion][80] so that it has sprung up independently as certain imperialistic practices in Europe. The states-men of Austria-Hungary have evolved the same kind of system.

Upon th[at] basis, [a Negro leader in the United States,][81] Mr. Booker Washington[,] took [and advocated] what he regards [as the existing system of bi-racialism, the] bi-racial organization of the Austro-Hungarian empire, and the solid—and the new—South. Now, that sys-tem is a system which has appealed to a great many practical statesmen today. Mr. Washington accepted it as a basis, as he thought, for con-structive work of race improvement in the South. He thought it neces-sary to take much of it and did so. He has been accused of creating it. He did not. He has been accused of confirming it. Perhaps, to an extent, he did, or has. But undoubtedly all he did as a practical con-structive worker was to realize that that was the basis of the social mind of the section[.][82]

[Time will be the] test of whether it is just. Now, certain statesmen abroad have fallen into the same position and practices in [attempting to adjust to the social mind of their nation.] At any rate they have based most of their [*constructive*] reforms upon the recognition of just this kind of policy in society. As a means of ultimate [survival] one must admit it is in certain periods apparently very necessary. I say that, hoping to be as impartial in this as I have tried to be in my former statements. The very fact, for example, that every constructive policy that has been proposed in Austria-Hungary for the last fifteen years has [*been consciously*] worked [out] upon this basis[, and] the fact that liberal and [conservative] states-men [in this country] [a]like should regard it as necessary for their reform platforms to admit possible bi-racial [social organization,] seems to indicate that there is something about it which makes [it] a natural [choice] to [a] practical [statesman] who wants to get things done, and who wants to leave the [ultimate][83] problems to the future for practical solution, seeing that they are impossible of practical solution imme-diately. They have therefore had to concede to this very prevalent opin-ion [on race matters; the] attitude [of] modern society [is that it] is ready to make considerable practical concessions in order to maintain a sem-blance of its apparent convictions upon the matter of race.

[Nevertheless,] the society that practices this bi-racial system pays a very dear price and is almost in the proverbial position of the man who "cuts off his nose to spite his face."[84] Yet so typical is this attitude of modern society that we must fancy that it has a good deal to do with conditions that are peculiarly modern, and I have tried to trace them to this situation[:] that modern society has been confronting two different sets of problems which we suggested in our last lecture—the economic and the social—and it is unwilling to make large concessions in both fields[.] And where it makes an economic concession, it wants a counter-balance of social stringency. Where it makes a social concession it wants a counter-balance of an economic stringency. You will find [that] all the handicaps [placed on] the colored peoples come under either one of these two areas.

[I have read a] letter where Carlyle is pointed out to have said that the attitude of the North to the Negro was: ["God] damn you and be free," and the attitude of the South to the Negro was: "God bless you and be a slave."[85] There is something paradoxical in the way in which society [regards minority] groups: [either they deny you economic freedom and remain] socially indifferent, [or they][86] give you economic [freedom] and social discrimination. Now, just what causes it is as yet beyond our comprehension. [But] it is a fact[,] and because it is a fact you can see just how this bi-racial theory or policy should spring up, particularly in the type of community that is forced by reason of economic cooperation to enlist the group in a joint economic activity, but that yet wishes to bolster its own contentions by social distinctions that run counter to the concessions that they have to make in an economic way.

The last fallacy—and I have [somewhat] changed the order—is that of automatic adjustment. Race distinctions are [partly] deliberate. Consequently[,] it is a mistake to regard them as automatic in their operation and as not subject to remedial measures. All [these fallacies are] false[,] but particularly this last fallacy[, because it] involve[s] false habits of judgment [as well as] false social standards. Now it is toward false social standards that our activity must be directed if we wish to controvert false race creed. Uphold the practice but controvert the standard, though if possible make society jointly controvert the standard. So that the standard in some way or other reaches the [point at][87] which [it upsets] the whole life of the society.

It was such a marvelous culmination of events which, for example, made the slavery question (which previously had been an economic issue and a sentimental and moral issue [for a small group of reformers]) [into][88] a vital question upon which society in America [had to][89] live or perish. Now that was because certain events brought the whole standard of the system into line with a practical issue. Wherever that can be done, the standard will be controverted[;] and really to the extent that certain practices and discriminations lead to such [a] challenge—an ultimate challenge of the standard—they are blessings in disguise, though they do not seem to be.

The final thing is that we shall see that human society must [*have*] a [*certain homogeneity based upon*] consciousness of kind, and that consciousness of kind is a healthy[,] and a normal[,] and a fundamental social instinct[.] But [we must remember] that this normal and healthy social instinct has a very abnormal expression from time to time in the false notions, the false conceptions[,] of kind which are not conceptions of social kind—not conceptions of civilization type, of the American civilization type—but [rather] conceptions of racial kind and conceptions of race type [as permanent and invariable.] Under certain circumstances[, however,] race types and race kind can be transformed [—the Semitic and the Negro peoples are examples—] into social kind[.][90] [R]eally and essentially a man must become one of the same race [or civilization type] when he lives or [*learns*] to live in the same civilization and [has] conformed to a civilization type. [This] is the only essential kind of race that exists in the world today.

In other words, if you have the same manners and customs and have allegiance to the same social system, you belong to the same race [or social kind,] even though ethnically you may not; so that really when you conform or belong to a civilization type, [(when you are an American in all your beliefs, mores, and social customs, for example)], you are of the same race in any vital or rational sense of race.[91] To exclude you from that kind of participation[,] to exclude you from that kind of race is simply arbitrary and [a] very perverse practice which comes from an abnormal conception on the part of the society of what consciousness of kind is and of what the social or civilization type consists.

So that prejudice[,] as far as we have traced it in this lecture[,] is simply an abnormal social sense, a [perversion] of a normal social instinct, which falsely attributes to certain arbitrary ethnological and biological factors, sociological and social standards which do not pertain to them at all, and which therefore operate to bring about the discrepancies which we confront when we see people who are on the way to conforming to the civilization type, denied participation and recognition in society, as if nothing mattered but their color or their kind.

NOTES: LECTURE 4

1. "pursued" replaces original "prosecuted".

2. Word deleted following "all": "that".

3. Phrase deleted following "irrational positions": "by reason".

4. Word deleted following "book": "on".

5. Evelyn Bering Cromer, *Ancient and Modern Imperialism* (London: John Murray, 1910), 128–43.

6. Paragraph break inserted at beginning of sentence.

7. Inaccurate phrase from quote deleted following "history": "[....] position which had [...] no basis".

8. Cromer, *Ancient and Modern Imperialism*, pp. 139–40. Additions to Locke quote supplied from this text.

9. Words deleted and word order changed. Original: "see certain dominant peoples to have come in possession of".

10. "[the related but]" replaces original "a [...] of".

11. "Because" deleted from beginning of sentence.

12. Word order changed. Original: "abnormal according not so much".

13. Word order changed. Original: "eradicating the social instincts upon which racial prejudice is based, from human society".

14. "not be able to rise above its" replaces original "but cannot rise superior to the".

15. "by" deleted following "force".

16. "finds to be" replaces original "is able".

17. Bacon's doctrine of the idols is developed in his *Novum Organum*, in aphorisms thirty-eight through sixty-nine. See *The Works of Francis Bacon*, collected and edited by James Spedding, Robert Ellis, and Douglas Heath (London: Longman and Co., 1860), vol. IV, *Translations of the Philosophical Works, vol. I The New Organon*, 53–70. Something of the analogy between Locke's view of the majority of racial conceptions and Bacon's idols is suggested by Bacon's thirty-eighth aphorism: "The idols and false notions which are now in possession of the human understanding, and have taken deep root therein, not only so beset men's minds that truth can hardly find entrance, but even after entrance [is] obtained, they will again in the very instauration of the sciences meet and trouble us, unless men being forewarned of the danger fortify themselves as far as may be against their assaults"(53). In Bacon Locke found an ally in his critique of pseudoscientific theorists who based their racial conclusions on a priori ideas, isolated instances, or theological traditions, rather than on patient scientific observation.

18. "and that" deleted following "groups".

19. Bacon's analysis of the idols of the theatre is developed in aphorisms forty-four, sixty-one, and sixty-two of *The New Organon*, 55, 62–64.

20. "Race antipathy" replaces original "it".

21. "It will" replaces original "which shall".

22. Word deleted following "Gallic": "and".

23. Tense changed and word deleted from original: "expresses itself in".

24. Word order changed. Original: "most virulent form [...] that cannot".

25. "that" replaces original "of".

26. David Schoenbaum provides a revealing analysis of ethnic tensions in the Alsace-Lorraine region in *Zabern 1913: Consensus Politics in Imperial Germany* (London: George Allen & Unwin, 1982), 71–114. Not only does Schoenbaum explicate how German occupation exacerbated indigenous ethnic tensions but also he shows how a German officer's use of an ethnic slur—calling Alsatians *Wackes* (or "niggers" in America's racial vocabulary)—was the spark that transformed smoldering tensions into the Zabern conflagration. See 98–103.

27. Locke may have been referring to the pre-World War I eastern province of Moravia, whose capital was Brunn. Brunn was later part of Czechoslovakia. I am indebted to Michael R. Winston for this suggestion.

28. "that" replaces original "it is just simply".

29. "even though" replaces original "but that".

30. Paragraph break at beginning of sentence is ignored.

31. Paragraph break inserted at beginning of sentence.

32. Word order changed. Original: "affair Dreyfus".

33. Alfred Dreyfus, a Jewish captain in the French Army, was court-martialed and convicted of treason in 1894 for reputedly selling French military secrets to the Germans. There was no actual evidence of Dreyfus's guilt but suspicion focused on Dreyfus because he was a Jew. For more information, see Nicholas Halasz, *Captain Dreyfus: The Story of a Mass Hysteria* (New York: Simon and Schuster, 1955).

34. "an analogy to the type of virulent Anti-Semitism we see in Europe. The flowering of prejudice against Negroes" replaces original "[....] and".

35. I have been unable to discover the incident on the evening of 17 April 1916 to which Locke refers here in the lecture. Perhaps Locke was referring to the student strike that had paralyzed Howard University, beginning in the second week of his lectures. The strike was nearly resolved by this evening's lecture.

36. See "Schmoller on Class Conflicts in General," a translation of remarks by Professor Schmoller appeared in *The American Journal of Sociology* vol. 20, no. 4 (July 1914–May 1915):504–31.

37. Locke may have been referring to Georg Simmel (1858–1918), although the facts of Simmel's tenure at the University of Berlin contradict Locke's recollection here. Simmel was a brilliant philosopher and an architect of modern sociology, who apparently introduced Locke to the discipline while he was a student at the University of Berlin from 1910 to 1911. Apparently because he was Jewish, Simmel had remained a *Privatdocent* until 1900. Nevertheless, Simmel was made professor of philosophy and sociology at the University of Berlin on 16 July 1900, well before Locke took classes from him. See Johannes Asen's *Gesamtverzeichnis des Lehrkorpers der Universitat Berlin, Bd. 1 1810–1945* (Leipzig: Otto Harrassowitz, 1955), 187. Simmel did leave the University of Berlin for an appointment as professor at the University of Strassburg on 1 April 1914, perhaps in response to mounting anti-Semitism in Berlin on the eve of World War I. The historian Fritz Ringer has suggested that Simmel's career was affected by anti-Semitism. See Ringer, *The Decline of the German Mandarins* (Cambridge: Harvard University Press, 1969), 136–37.

38. Irretreivable clause deleted following "professor": "[...] is forced to put a false basis of [...] philosophy."

39. "the most" replaces original "as much as".

40. "to observe that such" replaces original "[....] the".

41. "the" replaces original "so should their".

42. "and will continue to occur unless" replaces original "if".

43. "is" replaces original "cannot be".

44. The friend referred to was Horace Meyer Kallen (1882–1974), whom Locke had met at Harvard University, and who was an instructor at the University of Wisconsin from 1911 to 1918.

45. "[,]" replaces original "and".

46. Phrase deleted following "Now": "to get to terms in".

47. Fragment dropped from beginning of paragraph: "These interpolations are rather costly in time, but I think .... are a confirmation in my mind of this ...."

48. "sane" replaces original "save".

49. "prejudice" replaces original "it".

50. "react to" replaces original "treat with".

51. "react to" replaces original "treat with".

52. Edward Ross, "What are the causes of Race Superiority?" *Annals of the American Academy of Political and Social Science* 18 (July 1901):67–89. Reprinted in Edward Alsworth Ross, *Foundations of Sociology* (New York: Macmillan, 1912), 353–85.

53. Word order changed. Original: "people to be more successful who believe in it."

54. Words deleted following "successful": "and that".

55. Ignaz Zollschan (1877–1948) was an Austrian physician and anthropologist, who was moved by the racist writings of Houston Chamberlain, the British-born follower of Comte de Gobineau, to write *Das Rassenproblem Unter Besonderer Berucksichtigung der Theoretischen Grundlagen der Judischen Rassenfrage* (Vienna and Leipzig: W. Braumuller, 1912). This was Zollschan's most comprehensive work on race theory and probably the source of Locke's quotes. Zollschan was also a Zionist and wrote extensively on Jewish nationalism, including such works as *Jewish Questions: Three Lectures* (New York: Bloch Publishing Co., 1914) and *Die Revision des judischen nationalismus* (Vienna and Leipzig: W. Braumuller, 1920). In the 1930s, Zollschan responded to the Nazi mobilization by attempting to organize an international Society for the Scientific Investigation of the Racial Question. Taking up residence in London during World War II, Zollschan continued to write and produced, in *Racism Against Civilization* (London: The New Europe Publishing Co., 1942), an indictment of Nazi ideology. (*Encyclopedia Judaica* vol. 16 [New York: Macmillan, 1971], 1218.)

56. Word order changed. Original: "really—in Germany a great discovery was made—a discovery which was at the time invented".

57. "In particular" replaces original "Particularly".

58. For a discussion of Grimm's ideas of language and German national identity, see Peter F. Ganz's *Jacob Grimm's Conception of German Studies: An Inaugural Lecture Delivered Before the University of Oxford on 18 May 1973* by Peter Ganz (Oxford: Clarendon Press, 1973). Recent historians credit the German philologist F. Max Muller as the major mid-nineteenth-century figure who invented the concept of the Aryan language and with it the idea of the Aryan peoples. See Thomas F. Gossett, *Race: The History of an Idea in America* (Dallas: Southern Methodist University Press, 1963), 123–26. Eventually, Muller recanted his earlier contention that those who spoke the Indo-Germanic or Aryan languages belonged to an Aryan race. In his *Biographies of Words and the Home of the Aryas* (London, 1888), he stated that "I have declaried again and again that if I say Aryas, I mean neither blood nor bones, nor hair nor skull; I mean simply those who speak an Aryan language," (120).

59. "Grimm and other German philologists" replaces original "they".

60. "in practice" replaces original "practically".

61. Words deleted following "such": "that is to say,".

62. Paragraph break at beginning of sentence ignored.

63. Word order changed. Original: "[...] biological fallacy [....] a good deal of the race creed and theory of the present day."

64. Word deleted following "that": "the".

65. Locke may have been referring to Calvin Colton (1789–1857), the journalist and an advocate of colonization for Negroes in Liberia as a solution to the American race problem. Colton advanced an environmentalist explanation for the "deficiencies" in Negro character, believing that a change in the social conditions of life would improve black character. See his *The Americans* (London, 1833) and *Colonization and Abolition Contrasted* (Philadelphia, 1839). I have been unable to find the discussion of aggregates in Colton that Locke refers to in this passage.

66. Word order changed. Original: "and in the second place the proportionate rate of increase".

67. An example of this approach to the history of Greece is William Watkiss Lloyd's *The Age of Pericles: A History of the Politics and Arts of Greece*, vol. 2 (London: Macmillan and Co., 1875), 111–14, 117–19, 154–57, 178–85.

68. Paragraph break inserted at beginning of the sentence.

69. "its singlehanded" replaces original "the".

70. Franz Boas, *The Mind of Primitive Man*, with a new foreword by Melville Herskovits, rev. ed. (New York: Collier Books, 1963; orig. pub. 1911).

71. Word deleted following "that": "although".

72. Words deleted following "society": "and that".

73. Words deleted following "or": "as well as any".

74. Word deleted following "and": "that".

75. "term" replaces original "have".

76. "based on" replaces original "come from under".

77. "the lower standard of the group aggregate" replaces original "it".

78. "assimilation" replaces original "it".

79. "evidence" replaces original "question".

80. "this notion" replaces original "it".

81. "a Negro leader in the United States" replaces original "of which [....]".

82. Irretrievable clause deleted following "section": "and to use that to get what he repeatedly spoke of as the [...]".

83. "ultimate" replaces original "the merely [...]".

84. Paragraph break inserted at beginning of sentence.

85. I have been unable to locate any letter or other source for the remarks Locke attributes to Thomas Carlyle. Some of Carlyle's views on race relations can be found in his article, "The Nigger Question," in Thomas Carlyle, *Critical and Miscellaneous Essays in Five Volumes IV*, vol. 29 of *The Works of Thomas Carlyle in Thirty Volumes* 4 (New York: AMS Press, 1969), 348–83.

86. "or they" replaces original "and".

87. "point at" replaces original "issue by".

88. "into" replaces original "[...] led to the question of slavery becoming as it did,".

89. "had to" replaces original "must".

90. Words deleted following "kind": "and that".

91. Paragraph break inserted at the beginning of the sentence.

5

Racial Progress and Race Adjustment

L ADIES AND GENTLEMEN: There is a certain sense of the essential value of these things which comes over me particularly at this last lecture in the series. I am more than content with the way in which the subject has been developed. I feel that a hand has been put to [the subject] which has not been turned bac[k,] and we shall find at the conclusion of some years of these studies a peculiar satisfaction in these beginnings. The history of progress has been the history of the redemption of ideas, and the idea that we have been considering is one that stands very much in need of redemption, but one [in] which, I think, there are signs for us to believe that such a happy fate awaits it. It is always very encouraging to imagine the perfect revolution of attitude which comes about as soon as something which has been a mark or stigma becomes a mark of recognition. I suppose if the early Christian communities could have had their wish, the odious term "Christian" would have been blotted out of the vocabulary of men. And yet today it is the most worthy and the most indispensable name under which people are proud to be grouped and recognized.

Now there are too many of us (let us say too many people in the world, to put it broadly) who feel that race is so odious a term that it must be eradicated from our thinking and from our vocabulary. I believe that a word and an idea covering so indispensable[,][1] useful[,] and necessary a grouping in human society will never vanish, never be eradicated, and that the only possible way in which a change will come about

84

will be through a substitution of better meanings for the meanings which are now so current under the term. Really when we come to face the issue[,] we see that some of the most constructive thinking that has been going on within the last two decades has been in terms of units and ideas which really are racial in their very conception. Some of the most magnificent movements which have been recently inaugurated in art and in letters have taken their inspiration from the expression of racial idiom and race life. And certainly in those fields there has been a certain amount of redemption of the false social and economic meanings that have made the term rather a byword of reproach; [*how*] much of this that the cultural side of race will follow into race as a term of social living, we cannot at present say. It may not come through that channel, but most certainly the idea of race will be revolutionized in a very short while—within the lif[e,] perhaps[,] of this generation, or the next at the very outside[.] And we shall confront, then, [this]² last topic in a most hopeful and progressive frame of mind, one which should lead us to really our first constructive interpretation of race that we have permitted ourselves. Because all along, previously, we have been critical and not constructive.

Race as a unit of social thought is of permanent significance and of growing importance. It is not to be superceded except by some revised version of itself. Too much social thinking has gone into it for it to be abandoned as a center of thought or of practice. To redeem, to rescue, or [to] revise that thought and practice should be the aim of race theorists and those who want to educate people into better channels of group living.

The history of ideas of this kind is a history of a succession ³ ⟨⟨of meanings. What conception of race is to dominate in enlightened social thought and practice is the present problem. The sociological conception of race as representing phases, stages, and groupings in social culture repudiates the older biological and historical doctrines of race in social practice, although it does not wholly supercede them in their scientific uses.⟩⟩ [Eventually, modern anthropology will supply the] scientific notions of race [that] will take their places, their proper places, in scientific thought [and eventually in practical life and thought] to be superceded [later] in practical life and thought by other conceptions of race.

Let us review the senses of race that we have discriminated in the previous lectures. Physical race is, of course, the basic thing. "Pure race" it is often called[, and] by that I mean purity of blood. This we have found to be a scientific fiction. It is doubtful that any large amount of historical evidence can be cited to prove that it ever existed. It may have existed accidentally in certain primitive communities but quickly [was]⁴transformed as that group grew and progressed[.] So that it is something which practically mankind never [has]⁵ possessed but which if [it]⁶ did possess, [it]⁷ had to abandon in order to progress, in order to become civilized.

In other words, abandonment of pure or physical race seems to be one of the causes of civilization—a price that men have had to pay for their progress in social organization. If, then, [race purity]⁸ is something which has been rarely possessed, it is irretrievable[.] Surely it is something which we should not very much worry about from the practical point of view, and most of the doctrines of race integrity, doctrines which may be artificially stimulated and fostered by ideas of physical race, are simply unfortunate survivals of an older regime which never can be reinstated and a regime which the enlightened practices of society are likely to discourage as time goes on.

Personally[,] I became very interested in the eugenics movement when it was quite young. When Dr. [Francis Galton] founded the Society of Constructive Eugenics in London,⁹ [I became interested.] It seems to me that should any sound eugenic theory come into favor, the old votaries of physical race must undoubtedly go down in the path of its progress. But, be that as it may, pure race, physical race, has no meaning except in science, and then only from the point of view of certain anthropological classifications. Historically[,] race in the sense in which it is put (in which it was regarded in the second lecture) has been proved to be an anachronism. It is no longer necessary for social progress. In fact[,] it is something which is falsely attributed to the group as a race group. What men mean by "race" when they are proud of race, is not blood race, but that kind of national unity and national type which belongs properly not to the race but to the nation. If the nation should expand and incorporate other racial elements, the same kind of race type would undoubtedly be shared by people who really, biologically[,] have no connection with it, proving that a rational cult of a nation will never make the mistake of basing national type and civilization type upon a racial division.

That seems to be the tendency of nationalism everywhere, although some reactionary nationalism undoubtedly will be practiced for a long time yet in the categories of race. The only function of this historical conception of race is to justify the historical group sense and to stimulate men into that sense of corporate destiny which is, of course, an essential part of any healthy national unity. That much of race sense is healthy and to be regarded without fear because it performs a certain function[,] and in the light of that function[,] it must be admitted it is good. Politically[,] race and empire are practically staked upon the same issue, as I tried to demonstrate in my second lecture. We are somewhat doubtful about the future of race in the political sense. At present I think I showed that it was a considerable bulwark of the practice of empire as it exists today. Whether it is necessary to the existence and the maintenance of empire is possibly questionable. It seems from any rational point of view to be a mere policy or subterfuge of empire, which conceivably could abandon the false political sense of race and yet maintain itself. Whether that will be achieved, of course, is particularly the problem of the era of construction which will follow upon the great conflict in the midst of which we now are.

Social race is in a sense one of the most interesting aspects of race. Social race is perhaps also the oldest aspect of race. I had not time when we first mentioned it to go into its oldest reputed origin. It is said that the Indian cast[e] system represents perhaps the earliest known system of racial distinction, racial distinction in a social sense. Now if so, [if race has its][10] origin [in an ancient society organized] as caste, [then] we must think that social race is an anomalous thing today when society is universally organized upon what we know as a competitive industrial basis. The older origin was economic rather than a matter of blood, and the cast[e]s we differentiated as economic cast[e]s became, through the conservativism of Oriental life (particularly because of the religious distinctions that prevailed in the Hindu life)[,][11] forms of heredity. They do not represent races at all but simply economic castes that[12] bec[a]me hereditary through racial distinction, because of the peculiar kind of stagnant and separatist society which we have in the Orient. The men who followed a certain calling were confined in most of their [lives][13] to [be with] men of the same calling. [*Their*] [lives][14] therefore grew [and spread through descent] and marriage, of course, [and, in combination] with other institutional practices[,] tended speedily to transform an economic caste into a blood caste; and most authoritative students of Indian caste regard the blood cast[e]s as the result of the economic cast[e]s rather than vice versa. If that should be true, that the most arbitrary kind of caste we know of was not originally blood caste but produced by economic conditions, then it would seem obvious that a general economic condition which was counter to the economic condition which originally produced caste would in the end make caste impossible. And that is where I think we must pin a great deal of faith in the modern industrial and economic order.

As long as we have an industrial order which is competitive[15] (an order which seems to be spreading over the face of the globe)[,] we shall be able to regard caste as something which will be economically contradicted because, as you can see, a competitive industrial order means that one generation rarely occupies the same social position as the generation immediately before or after. In which case there must be not only change but there must be a constant process of transition in society, by which, according to a man's success, he promotes or demotes himself from one class to another. Since that process is vitally necessary to society[,] such a society is only going to maintain the caste spirit to the extent that such a system does not actually contradict [the successful functioning of the society.]

As you can see, basically, such a system does contradict it; and consequently[,] with the continuance of the industrial competitive system we shall see the gradual elimination, I fancy, of caste in the old sense. Of course, we cannot forecast what artificial limitations society may from time to time place upon this free movement within itself. Certain societies see the need to stabilize this from time to time by such artificial limitations, often imposing handicaps by which this process will be checked. But no such society could reasonably impose such limitations as would harm the society—that is to say, such limitations that would threaten to break up the society. The life of modern society is vitally at stake, then, with any retroactive limitation or measure that may be taken. Consequently[,] we may regard such a limitation or measure as something which will not go very far. The only kind of race that is left to believe in and to be applied to modern problems is what we call the idea of social race, defining it more narrowly as a conception of civilization type or civilization kind. This seems to be the only thoroughly rational meaning of race, and if one could venture a prophecy in what is supposedly a mere scientific treatment, it would be to say that this is to be the race concept of the future.

Every civilization produces its type. It either creates that type or molds it unless it is developed in some unexplained way[.][16] This seems to be a basic law in human society, that a civilization should produce a certain civilization type[,] that it should be judged in terms of that civilization type, and [that it] should come to know itself in proportion as it recognizes the type.

Now this recognition of type really imposes a very arbitrary and yet very natural obligation upon a man—conformity to the type. To conform to the civilization type is undoubtedly not only the duty but the burden of any man who wishes really to participate in it. Now, of course, it is a matter of considerable concern as to the degree of comformity necessary. Conformity may be of such a type that one would justifiably reject it. For example, if matters should come to[17] pass where religious conformity would be necessary to fully participate in society today, I fancy that we should be justified in saying[,] "Well, if that is the cost, if that is the price, it is too great." Yet, there has been a time when just such conformity was necessary, and if you were not of the same persuasion, if you were not of the same mind or faith, then there was practically nothing for you but persecution or exile.

Now, civilization is sometimes very arbitrary about the kind of conformity that it exacts, but at all times conformity to civilization type is the final social standard by which both the individual and the groups, the smaller groups, must be judged and must expect to be judged. Now what kind of conformity to civilization types does modern society exact? If[18] we can trace that, we have what is the crux of any so-called race problem. Because undoubtedly until we have traced any race problem to this factor, we have just touched the surface of it.

The essential thing amounts to this: In what kind of society do you wish to live? That "Do you wish to live?" is sometimes arbitrary[, for] it [often] means "In what kind of society were you born?" In what kind must you live? Let us leave it at that[:] In what kind of society must you live? Then the next question is: What is the civilization type prevailing there and how far do you as an individual (and how far does the group of which you are a constituent part) conform to that type? Because your participation will be gauged, will depend largely upon the conception that the general social mind places upon you individually and collectively with respect to what society deems to be its civilization type. It may be an arbitrary conception of [type,] but it is fair at least to the extent that it is apt to be the same standard that it imposes upon itself, [although] with the exception, of course, that any group that is only partially admitted will have to stand the burden of proof. Whereas, of course, for the fortunate group that comes in under what we might call the ethnic handicap, [that group] will have time to conform and will have all the help in conforming[;] whereas the other group will undoubtedly have the burden of proof upon it from the beginning.

Essentially, however, conformity to civilization type is something which society exacts of all its members. It is always arbitrary, sometimes more arbitrary than other [times], and in certain forms of society more arbitrary than in other forms. Consequently, we find in this the real crux of the problem.[19] Any individual or any lesser group than that of the nation must really see its problem as essentially a problem of conformity to the predominant and the prevailing civilization type. If it is prepared to work toward that conformity, either gradually or suddenly, it will find its recognition not lagging very far behind the actual evidences that it has faced that issue and met it successfully.

Now this conformity brings up the obvious problem of assimilation, which seems to be the [prime concern] of the sociologists who deal with these matters. Now I think to clear the situation we need only to distinguish between physical assimilation and cultural assimilation. They are not identical by any means, nor are they conditioned the one [by][20] the other. Undoubtedly[,] physical assimilation is conducive to a more rapid assimilation of the social culture wherever it is prevalent; but it is immaterial in the sense that it is not necessary. In fact, some of the most startling assimilations of social culture have taken place between groups that have not had any degree of physical assimilation.

I presume there never has been [greater] assimilation of social culture than that of the so-called Saracenic[21] [and the] Jew, yet there was never a time when the people of two racial groups were further apart from the point of view of physical amalgamation. The[22] assimilation of social culture, which we call for short, social assimilation[,] is necessitated by modern political and social organization. Ancient societies and oriental societies can tolerate a great divergency of social culture within their borders.[23] [In ancient society,][24] a man [was][25] free to follow [his][26] own tribal customs, rites, and social and political institutions[,][27] apparently only [to] live in one medley of tribes and nations under the hegemony of some more or less dominant political system. Just such an aggregation of people and of stocks constituted the Roman Empire, and before that, just such an aggregation constituted the earlier colonial empire of Greece and the Asiatic and African empires. We could scarcely credit the working possibility of such forms of social organization except for the constant reminder of the Orient today, where just such a practical cosmopolitanism seems possible without any way disintegrating the state system. You need only go to the Orient today to find conditions [akin to those] prevalent in ancient society, [E]astern and [W]estern[,] where there are apparently as many civilizations within one nation as we[28] have today (more in fact) than we have over the whole globe.

But under modern institutions undoubtedly that sort of thing seems to be impossible.[29] It seems that the very nature of the modern system and modern society is such that it cannot tolerate any great divergence in what we call the essential social conventions. By that I do not mean that modern society seems to exact of every man the same kind of religion or custom or what not[;] but I do mean that modern systems and modern society are so organized upon such a distinct principle of what we have defined as "civilization-type," that the only way to be a permanent factor in such a society is to exemplify that civilization type or to conform to it—to adopt it. Modern systems are system[s] that require or seem to require social assimilation. They are not necessarily so arbitrary about their social culture as the earlier societies were, but they are at least arbitrary to this extent: that in the interest of what they call a common standard of living, common institutions, and a common heritage, they exact that a man who elects, as an individual or [part of] a group, to live in a modern society must adopt, more or less wholesale, the fundamental or cardinal principles of that social culture.

That is what we mean when we say that America, for example, [is][30] "the melting pot."[31] Somebody said to Mr. [Israel] Zangw[i]ll: "You call America the melting pot. You ought to call America the bak[ing] oven, where your molten material is taken and absolutely baked into the most arbitrary forms."[32] It was a person who saw that back of the modern type of assimilation was a certain arbitrary conformity to type, and that America, for example, for all its boasted absorption of types, absorbs them only to re-make them or re-cast them into a national mold; and the essential basis of America's adoption is the re-working of the material into the type of the American citizen. Now American societies are of this sort—they have a very fixed and definite notion of their type, and to enjoy the privileges of such a society means to conform to that type. In most instances you welcome such conformity[, even with] the apparent inconsistency of inviting a man to disavow almost all that really should be dear to him, so much that a single [manifestation of ethnic identity] will [sometimes] bring [stigma to an individual or group. It is remarkable] that modern society is so essentially irrational that it [requires complete conformity to type.][33] To live in modern society means such an orthodoxy of living[,] as well as [such an] orthodoxy of social belief, that it seems[34] to threaten the freedom[,] the mental and moral freedom[,] of people.

Be that as it may, modern societies and civilizations are assimilative, and as assimilative societies [they] cannot tolerate any wide divergence of the social type. Now then, we are at a point where we can perhaps understand the way in which race issues have become so chronic today. They have become chronic because we are passing through a general phase of civilization in which there cannot be a great degree of social tolerance. Modern society boasts of its tolerance in certain matters [and,] in fact[,] it is very prone to boast [of] its superiority over medieval society, [*which,*] in the very nature of the case, had to exact religious conformity. Now if only the beam were out of our own eyes that we might see that with respect to another matter[,] we are just in the [same] position of the civilization of the medieval ages, [except][35] that the conformity which, it seems, modern society must exact is not conformity of belief but conformity of civilization type. There are very few shibboleths for this conformity other than those of race, but I want to call your attention to one of them, one that is sufficient, for example, in this country[,] to stir up racial antagonisms when no other artificial formula will do it. Go into any American community as an immigrant group, for example, and challenge what they call "the standard of living" and see what happens. Now just let any group of people do it if [it][36] dare. Let any group (Mongolian, Slavic, or from the same ethnic stock as the early American type) go into any American community and by their practices, economic or social, controvert what the American community calls its "standard of living." There [would be][37] an explosion[,] the same kind of an explosion that happened in medieval society when men of other faiths either invaded or cropped out to spoil the homogeneity of the orthodox religion of the community. Medieval [*society*] was very sensitive in those matters. Modern society is very sensitive in these other matters.

Professor Ross very distinctly says that whenever a modern society feels itself in jeopardy it does so in terms of what it calls its standard of living, which is partly an economic standard and partly a standard of what he calls the "national type."[38] Of course[,] one hopes that society in time will [move] into [that stage where it will be capable of] standing just these kinds of differences, in the same way that it has[,] through a painful [process] of history, been able to stand various persuasions of religious belief and practice. Until such social tolerance has been worked out, I fancy we shall be in the [same] painful position with respect to standard of living as medieval peoples were with respect to orthodoxy. [In modern] society [when conformity to type is construed] as [the] real standard of living, real institutional type is possible. That institutional type is not the culture of the dominant class merely. [It] really repre-sent[s] a composite type into which almost all elements of society must be [blended.] It is a process of real collaboration [of the races], a process in which, I fancy, racial adoptions and the assimilation of social culture by other groups perform on the whole a rather healthy and favorable function. Certain sociologists disagree with this, particularly that school which is represented by [Georges Vacher de] Lapouge,[39] who believes that alien races invariably have more or less an unfavorable influence. His sociological formula is the shibboleth of the man who believes in race inferiority and race integrity, for [LaPouge][40] says that it is always the lower race that prevails. Now, you can see that there is a good deal of common sense opinion that coincides with that school of social thought and that there is a good deal of instinctive belief that the man farthest down, for example, pulls the standard of living down with him[.] And [there is a good deal of instinctive belief] that the "alien," whether he be Caucasian or non-Caucasian, is a person whose influx in any great numbers will make the basis of society unstable and will tend toward the degeneration of social standards. "It is always the lower race that prevails."

Now there is a fundamental fallacy in that, a fallacy that we trace not so much in terms of practical examples as in simply trying to reason out what there is in social contact.[41] There are invariably two parties; and just as there must be two parties to a quarrel, there must be two parties to social contact. The stronger or dominant group is under the illusion that it controls its own social contacts[,] and that is an illusion. The stronger group, by virtue of the fact that it is stronger, has the power, the initiative, [but] that is all. The stronger group can no more deter-mine the rate or tendency of assimilation or amalgamation than a man can control his heartbeat. Not so much, [actually,] because a man can stop his own heartbeat, [but][42] the dominant group in society cannot stop the process of assimilation or amalgamation. They can check it[,] but they cannot stop it; and the reason is because[43] the real effective factor in race contacts resides in the will of individuals and the collective will of the alien group. Monsieur LaPouge is right to that extent, that it is invariably the alien group that has the final choice. And if[44] the alien group should decide to merge [totally with the dominant group,] nothing can stop [it].[45] It will be costly, [because,] for example, the alien group may be committing social suicide; but nothing on the part of the stronger group can prevent its doing so. Civilization type is such [a][46] thing that it is held up as a model. Any man who wishes to imitate it can do so. Society cannot maintain its exclusive standards and types free from imitation. In fact, it is [encouraging imitation] in making them exclusive, because to make a thing exclusive sets it up upon a pinnacle[,] and men's activities through assimilation are attracted toward it.

Consequently[,] the essential factor is the will of the alien group. If they will to assimilate, nothing on the part of the stronger group, of the dominant group, can do anything more than check it temporarily.

I should like to call your attention to certain instances which show, it seems to me, [that] social assimilation is [only][47] limited by the capacity for assimilation on the part of the alien group. The races with which the Caucasian people have recently come in[to] contact (by recently I mean a matter of several centuries) have been extraordinarily assimilative races. The two most noted are the Negro (as we conceive the Negro, that is to say that portion of the African stocks that through slavery has actually become incorporated in Caucasian societies) and the Japanese, who have not [been similiarly incorporated,] but who have come, within a few decades, into a very interesting contact with [W]estern peoples. Now both these peoples are both biologically and socially highly assimilative, highly adaptive through social assimilation.

The Japanese in their contact with [W]estern civilization have absorbed much, but under the pressure of a certain definite and well-controlled national policy they have made a reservation in favor of their own race practices, and have adopted, for the most part, only what we would call the utilities of modern civilization. This adoption of the utilities has somewhat transformed their civilization and altered it so that it isn't [exactly] the same Japanese civilization [that existed before Western contact. But Japanese social culture] is essentially what it was before contact with the [W]estern world[.] Only certain very practical utilities of [W]estern civilization seem to have been adopted and have had some modifying influence upon certain of their customs[.]

Now, the Negro has been denied the [positive] influence of any racial tradition [because of][48] slavery, which not only has cut him off from his tradition[s,] but which has engendered in him the attitude to repudiate it, even though, of course, some of the best efforts of the next generation must be toward reinstating what is honorable and what is really of value in that repudiated and artificially amputated past. As we see him in America, he makes absolutely no reservation. He is willing to conform to the very iota with the civilization type. And what is the consequence? The consequence has been a certain [negative] social reaction towards the Negro of which we have [spoken] in the preceding lecture. But as far as the social process of social assimilation is concerned,[49] the[50] measures which are being taken by a certain part of society [to segregate the Negro minority are having the] very contradictory [effect of] stimulating further assimilation[.] So that[, ironically,] American society is hastening the process of social assimilation by the very restrictive measures that [it is][51] imposing. From the point of view of social assimilation, the program of the American Negro seems to be absolute conformity to civilization type, [a] rather rapid conformity at that, [and] a wholesale adoption, [that is] almost too rapid an adoption for the healthy adjustment which should parallel it[.] But [this][52] process[53] prove[s my point] that the only way in which race assimilation can be effectively controlled is through the education of the group sense of the alien group. If anybody is interested[,] then[,] in directing the tendencies of social assimilation[,][54] he should aim to build[55] upon the minds of the alien group, instead of playing upon the minds of the dominant group, because [the alien group][56] is the seat of control, as I hope I have proved to you.[57]

Now the Anglo-Saxon race is in the present century in the paradoxical position of having made more contacts from a practical point of view [than any other group.][58] [The Anglo-Saxons][59] have brought about [social contacts between the most widely divergent groups in terms of their social culture]—divergences which have always existed before but which have never existed before under the same political [system. Some among the Anglo-Saxons have complained about this extraordinary race contact.] But their imperial [policies] have urged them on to bring this about[.] And [not surprisingly, social assimilation of the constituent groups has been difficult. The search is on for] a solution of the [problem, because it] is a solution which really vitally concerns the success of [Anglo-Saxon][60] civilization as much as it concerns the success of the constituent groups. Consequently[,] it is really a civilization problem [and] it is really an old problem [because social assimilation is] as vital to modern society as it is to any constituent race group. I[61] think we should show a disposition to share our race problems and to make them common problems of modern society. There is a good deal of talk of dividing this problem. There used to be talk of "the white man's burden," and now there is considerable talk of the black man's burden. I fancy possibly a few years will see a readjustment of that position—it is a common burden, a burden so common that perhaps only in a shifting of the issues can there be any really progressive adjustment. The concerns which the dominant groups have undertaken are concerns which they may ultimately have to cede to the (let us say) submerged groups or the [minority] groups; and the attempts which, for example, the Negro people have made toward construing their own problems may have to be revised, because some of the problems which we are trying to solve are not our problems at all but the projected problem of the troubled social issues and the social distinctions of the dominant group.

We spend a good deal of our time and our energy solving problems in that way. I fancy this is one reason why there is so much discussion and so little really constructive work upon certain race issues. The [black Americans] are engaged in debating the question from the other side of the house, you see, at present. Really that is paradoxical[:] ⟨⟨black Americans confront the most paradoxical situation, one that involves the ultimate⟩⟩ issue upon which race is to be confounded or converted, [and] the issue upon which race is going to be the salvation of modern society or its absolute confounding. Now, what is the issue? What is necessary? You will see from what I have said, that in the very nature of the case social imitation is to be the basis of any really sound progressive progress, and that social imitation is incumbent upon any alien group that considers itself integrally part of any national life. One must conform to the civilization type, but mere social imitation is, unfortunately, useless, for the reason that it involves antagonisms and reactions on the part of the dominant group that actually engender what we know as social friction.

While social assimilation is in progress there seems to be necessary some counter-theory, or rather some counter-doctrine. This counter-doctrine one finds in racial solidarity and culture. The stimulation of a secondary race consciousness within a group does seem necessary. It is necessary for several practical reasons. The group needs, in the first place, to get a right conception of itself, and it can only do that through the stimulation of pride in itself. Pride in itself is race pride, and race pride seems a rather different loyalty from the larger loyalty to the joint or common civilization type. Yet it is only apparently paradoxical. It is not paradoxical when it is worked out in practice, because, as has been pointed out, the very stimulation to collective activity which race pride or racial self-respect may give will issue into the qualification test and the aim to meet that qualification test, which, of course, must be in terms of the common standard. So that[62] through a doctrine of race solidarity and culture[,] you really accelerate and stimulate the alien group to a rather more rapid assimilation of the social culture, the general social culture, than would be otherwise possible.

This race pride or secondary race consciousness seems to be the social equivalent to self-respect in the individual moral life. I haven't time to dwell upon that, I merely mention it as the closest analogy I can find for it. It is a doctrine peculiarly [appropriate] to this generation of the Afro-American. I fancy he should feel more disposed to accept a better attitude [toward race consciousness. Such race consciousness] has been a feature of national revivals in European politics and European art in the last generation[, especially] in the Celtic, Provencal, and Polish revivals in art[s] and letters[, and in] political propaganda for recognition [of the right to self-determination for both] Ireland and Poland. [These movements] have been just this sort of consciousness within the larger national group of which they are really recognized as a constituent part. [They have been even more] recognized [as] a constituent part than we[,] because, for example, the Pole is recognized in Russian culture[;] and the thing that he is fighting [for] is [the right to determine] just what [kind of] recognition [he receives]. He doesn't want to be recognized until he is recognized in terms of his own estimate of himself[;] and to do that [the Poles][63] have had to institute a counter-doctrine and [to express][64] Polish nationality under the [Russian hegemony,] motivated by the desire for Polish autonomy or popular self-government. [The Poles want to be] free to maintain and to operate what is best and noblest in their cultural tradition[,] and for the purpose of maintaining their own traditions and practices[,] they have found it necessary to re-create the national type.

Now[65] for what purpose will we similarly find it necessary to re-create the race type?[66] [We will find it necessary o]nly for the purpose ultimately to merge it with the general civilization type. I fancy that we can only get recognition for our [contribution] collectively [and only][67] through a recognition which is almost instinctively given a re-created race type that expresses itself in terms of a representative class or representative products. At any rate, even should the final recognition not come in terms of a re-created race type, surely for the purpose of the stimulation of the assimilation of social culture, the secondary race consciousness and its development seems necessary.

This secondary race consciousness and all that it implies does several things.[68] In the first place, it prevents the representative classes, as they develop[, from] being merged[, really absorbed][69] into the larger group,[70] from being dissipated and lost in the larger group[.] And it also has the practical advantage of harnessing them to the submerged group, which stimulates, of course, the general progress [of the group,] even though it may appear temporarily to check the progress of the surface class[.][71] [T]he representative class invariably, of course, [is the first to] come to the surface, from the point of view of contact. Now this is not a doctrine of race isolation. It is not even a doctrine of race integrity. It is really a theory of social conservation which in practice conserves the best in each group, and promotes the development of social solidarity out of heterogeneous elements.

Such a doctrine sets up [a dam in the social] stream that gradually is raised [as the representative classes] lift the submerged class until its volume [reaches the general level of society as a whole.][72] Constant communication is necessary, and though this doctrine seems to recognize an artificial barrier between the two groups, that barrier is not placed between the source of supply and the social reservoir, but rather between a certain portion of society[73] [and the general society as a whole. It doesn't stop the] social [inflow from the larger society,] and [yet it does restrict] outlet [of group talent]. It doesn't stop access to the supply of the [larger] civilization, but it does stop the egress [from the group] until such a time as a submerged level can be brought up to the general level, which seems necessary for an effective outlet and an effective [in]flow. It is a process by which a representative product is accumulated. It is a process of artificial restriction perhaps of social outlets until such a time as [the representative classes][74] can [buoy the entire group] from their volume and bring up the mass to a certain requisite level. This necessity for damming up the social stream seems really necessary[,] and I only wish to indicate this interpretation of the doctrine because it seems to me it has been seriously misconstrued as it has been promulgated among us in this country. Now this is wholly apart from whatever methods [of propaganda] have made necessary the promulgation [of an argument to justify segregation in the minds] of the American public. The American public, whether it is interpreted in Washington rightly or not, has become very generally convinced of this doctrine of what it construes to be race integrity, race solidarity, race within the nation, each race for itself, and so on. It has its own motives for believing that. [The American public][75] is willing to pay considerably to have that propaganda more widely spread than it is at present even. It would seem to be falling in line with that doctrine to advocate the doctrine of race conservation, or rather the doctrine of social conservation which we have propounded. I merely want to hint that there is possible a wide difference between these two theories even though for the time they may seem to amount to practically the same thing. It is rather in the better construction, or reconstruction of policy that I think most of our constructive race measures will be[76] undertaken in the future.

And now just a final word about what really is the goal of race progress and race adjustment. The thing which it must promote if the concept of social race and civilization-type is to prevail (and I think it must ultimately) is culture-citizenship. Now, culture-citizenship is something which is to be acquired through social assimilation, not necessarily physical assimilation[.] It is a thing which is not acquired merely in terms of social [mixing of groups or] civilization merely. ⟨⟨Culture-citizenship⟩⟩[77] must come in terms of group contribution to what becomes a joint civilization. [That][78] is where the consummation of the doctrine that I have just mentioned will be found, because it will enable us[,] and others who have the burden of social proof placed upon them, to qualify in terms not merely of imitation but of contribution.

Until alien [group talents and] certain representative products are developed (which products for their sheer intrinsic worth are worthy of incorporation into the joint culture), I fancy no really final and satisfactory race recognition will be accorded[.] And certainly an idealized [though] soundly-based doctrine of the type that we have expressed will be necessary for the production of any racial contribution such as may gain us that type of recognition.

The prologue of political recognition of submerged nationalities in Europe has been their separate struggle for artistic expression—a recognition in music, in the arts (I mean the plastic arts), and in the representative arts [of] letters. The Celtic[79] [and] the Pan-Slavic movement[s] in arts and letters—movements by which the submerged classes are coming to their expression in art—seem to be the forerunners of that kind of recognition which they are ultimately striving for, namely, recognition [of an] economic, [a] civic, and [a] social sort; and these [movements] are the gateways through which culture-citizenship can be finally reached.

Culture-citizenship is the thing.[80] It is the goal in which we can jointly accept whatever [of value] there is in the civilization's conception of itself.[81] With the development and education of a higher type of race consciousness, race type blends into the "civilization type," and when the race type blends into the civilization type[,] the race issue has not only been solved[,] but the race issue has performed a social function in society because it has blended two heterogeneous elements into a homogeneity of which [n]either one in itself would have been incapable without the collaboration and the help of the other.

Race progress and race adjustment must, it seems to me, achieve this end. Whatever theory [or][82] practice [moves][83] toward it is sound; whatever opposes and retards it is false.

This is the very encouraging and finally acceptable theory of race with an equivalent practice that my study of these matters has brought me to. I do not ask your acceptance of it, but I do bring it forward as something which has not been foreseen, or rather was not foreseen when I started out in an attempt merely to survey scientifically the ground that we have now covered. I want to thank you for your cooperation and attention, which has made it possible for me to do this thinking. There is a certain amount of thinking that is possible within the four walls of one's study, but anything which so vitally affects the practical issues of life must be thought out in terms of the living world and must be thought out with the cooperation of other minds. [And I have sought] to bring these thoughts, after they reached a certain point or stage, to you, and you have seen them fashioning themselves to meet your receptive impressions. I want to thank you for it because my ultimate aim is simply to arrive at what may be in final form a presentment of this question which shall more or less redeem the subject from the debates of adherents to mere partisan doctrine. We wish to arrive at a wholesome, sound, and scientific consideration of matters that must be discussed but that we cannot much longer tolerate to be discussed in the way and on the plane that public discussion usually takes[.] And it is toward the redemption of that kind of discussion of the race questions[,] as well as[84] bringing a little nearer these rather better conceptions of race[,] that I have been impelled, with your cooperation, to make this attempt.

NOTES: LECTURE 5

1. Word deleted following "indispensable": "and".

2. "this" replaces original "that".

3. The text of page four, after "succession," is missing from the transcription in the Alain Locke Papers at Howard University.

4. "was" replaces original "to be".

5. "has" replaces original "have".

6. "it" replaces original "they".

7. "it" replaces original "they".

8. "race purity" replaces original "it".

9. I am unable to find evidence of the Society for Constructive Eugenics to which Locke refers, but it seems likely that Locke meant the Eugenics Education Society (EES) that was formed in London in 1907–8 as an offshoot of the Moral Education League. This society, which published *The Eugenics Review* from 1909 to 1968, popularized human genetics as a means of improving the racial quality of the British population. The society sought to carry on the work of Sir Francis Galton (1822–1911), the statistician and self-trained anthropologist, whose book, *Inquires into Human Faculty and Its Development* (London: J. M. Dent and Sons, 1884), introduced the word eugenics. Galton founded the Francis Galton Eugenics Laboratory at the University of London at University College but he was not the founder of the EES: no single person was. Moreover, the EES may have been a rival to Galton's laboratory. Nevertheless, Galton was the man known throughout England as the founder of the modern day eugenics movement, which was acknowledged, somewhat begrudgingly, in the first issue of *Eugenics Review*. In the absence of any other well-known "founder" to whom Locke may have referred, I have inserted Galton's name in brackets (although he was not a doctor) and retained Locke's title for the Society on the chance that such an organization did exist. Most likely, Locke misremembered the title of the organization and associated Galton's name with the organization, as well as the movement. (G. R. Searle, *Eugenics and Politics in Britain, 1900–1914* (Leyden: Noordhoff International Publishing, 1976), 1–19; *The Eugenics Review* 1 (April 1909–January 1910):14; *The Eugenics Review* 60 (March 1968):1–24.)

10. "if race has its" replaces original "any terms of this".

11. Word deleted following "life": "because".

12. Word order changed. Original: "that because of the peculiar kind of stagnant and separatist [...] society which we have in the Orient, become hereditary through racial distinctions."

13. "lives" replaces original "life".

14. "lives" replaces original "life".

15. Clause deleted following "competitive": "and of the kind which we have".

16. Word deleted following "way": "developed".

17. Word deleted following "to": "the".

18. Word deleted from beginning of sentence: "Because".

19. Paragraph break following "problem" ignored; sentence fragment dropped from end of sentence following "problem": "Now, according to their social affiliations and contacts, it seems to me—according to the social environment to which they as a group and as individuals must adjust themselves [...]."

20. "by" replaces original "on".

21. Saracenic is the adjective for the Saracens, the ancient name for the "nomadic peoples of the Syro-Arabian desert which harassed the Syrian confines of the Empire; hence, an Arab." (*Oxford English Dictionary* vol. 9 (Oxford: Clarendon Press, 1970), 106.) Here Locke may have been referring to the Moorish occupation of Spain, circa 705–715, that followed the Christian rule of Spain when Jews were enslaved, forced to follow the Christian faith and to intermarry with Christians. Under the Moorish occupation, by contrast, Jews were allowed to follow their own religion, and a golden period of cultural borrowing and exchange between Jews, Moors, and Christians ensued. See Ameer Ali, *A Short History of the Saracens* (1890; reprint, London: Macmillan, 1924), 107–20. For a more contemporary view, see S. M. Imamuddin, *Some Aspects of the Socio-Economic and Cultural History of Muslim Spain, 711–1492 A.D.* (Leiden: E. J. Brill, 1965).

22. Word order changed from original: "Social assimilation, which we call for short, the assimilation of social culture, is necessitated by modern political and social organization."

23. Sentence that followed "Ancient societies . . . borders" shifted to end of paragraph and broken into two sentences, with word order changes from the original: "You need only go to the Orient today to find conditions prevalent in [. . .] ancient society, eastern and western where there are apparently as many civilizations within one nation—as we today have—more in fact—than we have over the whole globe."

24. "In ancient society" replaces original "Where".

25. "was" replaces original "is".

26. "his" replaces original "their".

27. Word order changed. Original: "institutions only apparently".

28. Word order changed. Original: "we today have".

29. Paragraph break inserted at beginning of sentence.

30. "is" replaces original "as".

31. Paragraph break inserted at beginning of sentence.

32. Israel Zangwill (1864–1926) was an Anglo-Jewish novelist, essayist, and playwright, who is best known for his play, *The Melting-Pot: Drama in Four Acts* (New York: Macmillan, 1932; orig. pub. 1914), that opened on Broadway in 1908. That play chronicled the pain and anguish of assimilation and generational conflict for a Jewish family living in New York City. Although a Zionist for much of his life, Zangwill had reached the conclusion in the early 1900s that the only resolution of Jewish double identity—and double consciousness—lay in the complete absorption of the Jewish ethnic identity into the national identity of the American. The play's title became a popular metaphor of the expectation that European immigrants coming to the United States would abandon their traditional cultures and assimilate totally American values and culture. I have not been able to find the "somebody" Locke suggests confronted Zangwill or the source of Locke's quote. But Joseph H. Udelson's recent study of Zangwill provides an excellent discussion of the kind of issues Locke raised in this passage. See Joseph H. Udelson, *Dreamer of the Ghetto: the Life and Works of Israel Zangwill* (Tuscaloosa: University of Alabama Press, 1990), 194–99, and especially 237–51, where Udelson provides a comparative analysis of Zangwill's and W. E. B. Du Bois's views on cultural assimilation.

33. "requires complete conformity to type" replaces original "takes [....]".

34. Phrase deleted following "seems": "to him".

35. "except" replaces original "but that".

36. "it" replaces original "they".

37. "would be" replaces original "is".

38. A discussion of the "standard of living" by Edward A. Ross (1866–1951) can be found in his *Social Psychology: An Outline and Source Book* (New York: Macmillan Co., 1912), 262–70.

39. Georges Vacher de Lapouge (1854–1936) was a member of the French nobility, who as a thinker was obsessed with the significance of heredity as a factor in social life. Born near Poiters in central France, Lapouge attended the Lyceum, where he studied philosophy; later, he studied medicine and the law in Paris, took examinations in Egyptology, Hebrew, Chinese, and Japanese, and studied natural history. After receiving a doctorate of law in 1879, Lapouge worked only briefly as a district attorney in 1883, before spending the rest of his life in various university and library positions that allowed him in time for natural history research and writing. A stint as a librarian at the University of Montpellier in 1885 allowed him to lecture and conduct research on anthropology. That research formed the basis for his major works, *Les selections, sociales: cours litre de science politique* (Paris: A. Fontemoing, 1896) and *L'Aryen: son role social* (Paris: A. Fontemoing, 1899). Lapouge's views blended together ideas from Count Gobineau and Charles Darwin. Lapouge believed that biology had much to teach the social sciences. But where Darwin was tentative and skeptical about such applications, Lapouge made sweeping conclusions about the presumed biological basis for civilization's progress and decline. Like Gobineau, Lapouge believed that race mixing was the key to the success or failure of a people. But whereas Gobineau believed that some race mixing was good for a nation, Lapouge held that it was always bad, particularly when it occurred between Nordics and non-Nordics. Even more, Lapouge developed specific recommendations to legally prohibit race mixing to encourage (and protect) the production of the "higher races." "Inferiors," he believed, should be quarantined and allowed to die off; when reproducing, they should be castrated and when ill, they should be denied medical help. On the other hand, healthy women of the "higher races" should be compelled by law to breed as part of a compulsory motherhood service. When healthy women had difficulty conceiving, Lapouge recommended artificial insemination, and he claimed later that he was the first to advocate that procedure. Lapouge's greatest enmity was reserved for the Jews, who he believed were sneaky and totally objectionable as a people. Lapouge lived to see the beginnings of the Nazi insitutionalization of his views in the 1930s. Three years after his death, his book, *L'Aryen* was translated into German.(Gunter Nagel, *Georges Vacher de Lapouge (1854–1936): Ein Beitrag zur Geschicte des Sozialdarwinismus in Frankreich* (Freiburg: Hans Ferdinand Schultz, 1975), 4–62.)

40. "Lapouge" replaces original "he".

41. Paragraph break inserted at beginning of sentence.

42. "but" replaces original "and".

43. Word order changed. Original: "and the reason is because [. . .] in the will of individuals and the collective will of the alien group resides the real effective factor in race contacts."

44. Words deleted following "And if": "its choice, for example, should run to low—if for example".

45. "it" replaces original "them".

46. "a" replaces original "an [. . .] such an".

47. "only" replaces original "simply".

48. "because of" replaces original "through".

49. Phrase deleted following "concerned": "there is apparently".

50. Phrase "very contradictory measures" that followed "the" in original moved to middle of sentence.

51. "it is" replaces original "they are".

52. "this" replaces original "a".

53. Phrase deleted following "process": "which should".

54. Word order changed. Original: "assimilation, instead of playing upon the minds of the dominant group he should aim to build upon the minds of the alien group, because there is the seat of control."

55. Word deleted following "build": "play".

56. "the alien group" replaces original "there".

57. Irretrievable sentence fragment deleted following "you": "Under the best construction of the laws of social imitation, which, of course, are well known as those of the [....] Tarde."

58. Paragraph break inserted at beginning of sentence.

59. "The Anglo-Saxons" replaces original "[...] which is the a [...] of the century [...]".

60. "Anglo-Saxon" replaces original "their".

61. "Consequently" dropped from beginning of sentence.

62. Word order changed. Original: "So that you really through the means of a doctrine of race solidarity and culture accelerate".

63. "the Poles" replaces original "they".

64. "to express" replaces original "the expression of".

65. Word order changed. Original: "Now we will similarly find it necessary to recreate the race type for what purpose?"

66. Paragraph break inserted at beginning of sentence.

67. "and only" replaces original "approximation toward the civilization type".

68. Paragraph break inserted at beginning of sentence.

69. "really absorbed" replaces original "anticipated".

70. Phrase deleted following "group": "and here I must ask your indulgence to read a passage [...]". Word order changed. Original: "passage—it not only does that but it harnesses them in the service of the submerged group. In other words it is a [...] which prevents your representative classes as they develop being dissipated and lost in the larger group."

71. Word deleted following "class": "because".

72. Paragraph break inserted at beginning of sentence.

73. Phrase deleted following "society [...]": "or of" .

74. "the representative classes" replaces original "they".

75. "The American public" replaces original "it".

76. Word order changed. Original: "will be in the future undertaken".

77. "Culture-citizenship" replaces original "it".

78. "That" replaces original "There".

79. Words deleted following "Celtic": "movement in art and letters".

80. Paragraph break inserted at beginning of sentence.

81. Irretrievable sentence fragment deleted after "itself": "In which we must in [. . .] some extent [. . .] to which we must in greater extent conform, and it seems to me [. . .] in the community's ideal aspects we can very well afford to agree."

82. "or" replaces original "and".

83. "moves" replaces "makes".

84. Word deleted following "as": "the".

Appendix:
The Great Disillusionment*

The nineteenth century, despite the materialism of its progress and civilization achievements, was[,] in matters of[1] theory and justification, a century of magnificent idealisms—idealisms that may appear in the light of the events of the twentieth century to have been magnificent illusions. Thrice and four times blessed are the apostles of moral evolution who have been spared the great disillusionment, for as nothing short of this can a reflective mind rate the events of this eventful year. It is not a mere matter of history repeating itself, with a strange reversal of roles [such that] Europe[,] politically[,] stands again at the point where she stood in 1814[.] It is more serious than if the clock of time had slipped back a century[.] For history is no longer mere history[:] the nineteenth century taught us to call it progress and to count each calendar year as so much moral gain. So that it is the wheel of progress as well as the clock of time that has slipped a cog and turned back.

Progress turning backward! Truly a great disillusionment, yet biological evolution from which we drew the analogy should have taught us that there was many a backward turning and many a cul de sac in the road of even physical development[.][2] Goethe, foreseeing the danger of a straight-line theory of progress, gave a sage warning when he compromised on a spiral. But are we[,] even in the course of human events,

*This lecture was delivered by Alain Locke to the Yonkers Negro Society for Historical Research in Yonkers, New York on September 26, 1914. Locke had recently returned from Europe, where he witnessed German and English mobilization for World War I.

at the same juncture but on a higher plane from that in which we were in 1814? The issues are different[,] the alignment is different[, and] certainly the science of the intervening century has revolutionized the means and methods. But the ends! What of the ends?

The moral ends of the present day conflict, taking them at their best rather than at their worst, are, be it said with all reverence, no whit better and but little different from those of a century ago. Despite the fact that the struggle for existence has been mitigated and mankind is less than ever compelled by his environment to prey upon his own species, factors admittedly within man's control, his deliberate aims and ambitions have again forced the situation where the earth is not large enough for rival strong men and rival nations. And strangely enough the struggle has broken out at the heart of the great European civilization, rather than at its extremities—that is a fact to be marveled at, with worlds yet to be conquered in the sense of being civilized. With Asia yet [unconquered] and Africa really unconquered, the quarrel has broken out not over what both covet and neither has, but over what one has and the other envies, or stricter still[, over] what one has and the other threatens to take away. Further, [the] world's statesmen, who have not shamed to use the loftiest idealisms of social philosophy as a mask for their mutual enmity and hostile preparations, have finally dropped their masks and confessed that all pretexts aside, the real cause, and the real issue is a war to the death rivalry between two arms of the same civilization[,] the same race. With Gallic civilization as a dueling ground, Anglo-Saxon civilization is engaged in a duel to the death.

My friends[,][3] I am too sensible of our personal and racial debt to European civilization and culture to use this inopportune moment to put it to disadvantage, but for years, indeed in my first communication to this society in 1911[,] I distinctly claimed that we should be prouder as a people of having acquired this civilization and culture than of having it as an inheritance. I said this first in the interests of sincerity[.] I thought our culture would be sounder if we made no false claims to it, and had a sense of our own racial and ethnical past as a foundation upon which to rear it[.] But now not merely for our own pride's sake[,] but to avoid their shame, let us realize and confess that the civilization which is at war with itself is not ours in the intimate sense that we owe it a blood debt or even an irrevocable allegiance.

Indeed one of the predictable results of the war will be its inevitable lesson to other races and alien civilizations that I trust will forever make impossible the Frankenstein of the nineteenth century—the pretensions of European civilization to world-dominance and eternal superiority. Grant it cheerfully its little day, subtle sons of Asia and patient children of Africa, grant it its due in the beneficial spread of a certain kind of civilization, a certain energizing of the stagnant world of other continents, grant it even its century or so more of dominance and pride (and another century for good measure, as I am not so foolish as to believe European civilization at the crumbling point in this crisis)[,] but withal learn the lesson that[,] like a handwriting on the wall, suddenly looms up out of our darkness before us.[4]

So many are awaiting actual results—what will be the outcome of this fearful struggle?—without realizing that the mere outbreak of the war is the greatest fact. What is the greatest result of the war [is] the war itself [:] certain conclusions are already as apparent as they are inevitable[.] Here is an instance where philosophers like prophets can be wise before the event[.] Anglo-Saxon civilization, in its spread and pretensions, could not be the possession of a single nation, though she has been the brunt of it and furnished the ideal[.] England was forced to take the rest of Europe into a sort of limited partnership. As modern imperialism came more and more to be a racial matter, the philosopher and statesmen were forced, even in view of their bitter rivalries, to assert the co-partnership of European nations[.] And from Germany[,] the greatest rival[,] came the strongest proofs of the racial bond in the compact—Anglo-Saxon predominance, Teutonic superiority, and what not.

One of the moments of my life will be hearing one of the greatest apostles of this idea announce the dissolution of this partnership.[5] Up to a few days ago England[,] America[,] and Germany were custodians of Anglo-Saxon civilization[.] Now before the youngest as a neutral spectator, the elder partners struggle in [a] death-grip, one treacherously inviting the assistance of the civilization that has threatened us a thousand years—the Byzantine, Slavic oriental culture—[and thereby is] willing to pull the house over its head if it cannot win its feud by any other means.

The venerable scholar burst into tears, and bowed his head.[6] The Anglo-Saxon partnership dissolved! It does not mean the end of the enterprise, but it does mean the lapse of the old charter, the divine right of certain nations to govern others. For whichever nation that wins[,] empire can no longer mean the God-given privilege to rule the world[.] The imperial pretensions of a whole race perished therefore with the quarrel.

Many will dispute the fact that the imperial rivalry is the ground cause of the present conflict, particularly the rivalry as between two arms of the Teutonic race, the Germans and the Britons. But an examination can as easily substantiate this claim as well now as history must later. To my mind the most certain proof that this is [the] main issue between Germany and Great Britain is the hysterical assertion of each that they are fighting for the same thing. "We fight for civilization." Civilization in that sense is no national ideal, even in the hysteria of war propaganda. It is not a conflict over differing aims or systems. It is a quarrel over a leadership that only one can exercise. This is the essence of the imperial idea: it is not as nations but as empires that Germany and Britain rival each other.

Further still, what lies back of the most commonly asserted cause, militarism, with its complement of navalism, are in their modern forms a product of empire, and it is simply a question [of] which is the most efficient agent, the weapon of conquest or the weapon of maintenance, physical force or material resources[?][7] Again what is[8] Germany['s] sponsorship for Austria, but the tutelage of a younger and more unsuccessful accomplice at the imperial game. What is Russia's shibboleth, the Pan-Slavic idea—another imperial scheme. This is a war of empires, though the irony of it is that the actual brunt of suffering is borne by countries like Belgium and France, nations [still][9] despite their vicious attempts at Empire under their Anglo-Saxon tutors. Many have said the war is a war of cliques, of emperors and dynasties. It would be nearer the truth to say it was a war of peoples—a race war—but truest of all, and worst of all, it is a war of ideas, for the utopia of empire and the dream of an unlimited and permanent overlordship.

Trace this idea to its source[,] and you will find the novel cause of the present war. Historians will be busy at this particular task for generations, no doubt, and there is for our small purposes, little need to anticipate them. The burden once settled on imperialism will be visited no doubt upon the Romans, the Greeks, the Persians, [and] the Chaldeans in turn as history traces the root of the evil back in its endless progression. But though there is little cause and smaller profit in discovering who invented the notion of empire, the source is quite clear from which it has flowed into modern politics and corrupted the very patrimony of the race that has professed it.

Let me quote the remarkably frank and clear-sighted statements of the North American last month,[10] (page 322; page 330):

Europe's narrow boundaries have not sufficed a moment for the insatiable appetites of its children, and from the broad quays of its busy ports number-less merchantmen have sailed forth to scour the seas for markets and have returned laden with the produce of the Orient and the New World. No quarter of the earth has been too barbarous or remote to escape the ambition of its colonists, and every unclaimed region of the globe has long since been pre-empted for one or other of its rival flags. Africa and the far-off archipelagoes of the Pacific are wholly under European sway. Only the extreme of Orient has succeeded in guarding its political identity, while Latin America, though maintaining its freedom, has become one of the richest fields for European economic exploitation. To outward seeming Europe has become the master of the world.

Yet beneath this fair exterior of power and glory a canker has long eaten into Europe's very heart—the canker of jealousy and internecine hatred, which threatens to pull all in jeopardy and which menaces its warring children with a sudden fall to the dead level of a common ruin. . . . That mad piling up of fleet upon fleet and army upon army against which so much rhetoric has been expended these later years has been but the most striking symptom of a disease curable only by fundamental change in the European state of mind, a malady which no machinery of arbitration could reach—only the conversion of the European soul.[11]

Consider also the momentous social possibilities involved in the Great War. The existing social order may break down utterly beneath the fright-ful strain; the governments, in a combined military and financial bank-ruptcy before the sudden attack of a desperate, hunger-stricken proletariat already fired by the Syndicalist gospel of violent social revolution, and the old Europe may disappear in a welter of anarchy. On the other hand, bloodshed and battle may intensify national consciousness of the Eu-ropean peoples, deepen the hatreds between race and race, plunge the world into a whole cycle of wars—a new Iron Age in which the finer flowers of our civilization would be ruthlessly trampled under foot, and the present era of free thought and individual liberty be replaced by the hand of military despotism.

Again, consider the possible reactions of this European conflagration upon the world at large. Up to a month ago the white race was master of this planet. Africa was absolutely beneath European sway, while in Asia only the island Empire of Japan had made good its position, and this only by the grace of European disunion and the alliance of the European British Empire. But in these last ten years a strange breath has passed over the Asiatic world. The victories of Japan have awakened the dormant spirit of the East, and the countless millions of the Orient, once so passive, to chafe sullenly at the European yoke. India is seething with unrest at the British "Raj"; "un-changing" China is changing at last, and their teeming populations are beating fiercely against the white man's own frontier and answering his exclusion laws with threats and menaces which portend still mightier race struggles in the years to come—struggles beside which even the present battle of the nations might seem tame indeed.[12]

After this who will doubt that the trouble is a war of races. A racial feud has been smoldering under the surface of European civilization these centuries. It will be evident how foolish it is in the light of these facts to regard the rivalries as merely political, involving merely the personal ambitions of rulers, or the designs of contending bureaucracies. In each country the common folk feel their existence is in jeopardy. Possessing often a common culture and tradition, they are nevertheless forced to regard themselves as bitterly estranged. The epithet of barbarian and enemy of civilization is hurled at blood brothers[;] the idea of Empire, the nemesis of alien races, has turned upon its authors.

NOTES: DISILLUSIONMENT

1. Word deleted following "of": "the".
2. Word deleted following "development": "and".
3. "Y. Society only-" in Locke's hand above "My friends" on the page 5 in the Alain Locke Papers at Howard University. Locke may have intended to publish an edited version of this lecture in *The North American Review*. See next note.
4. Sentence fragment deleted after "before us." Original: (substitute paragraph-for the N. Amer. article in end.) way in which this result will contradict the ends of both in mature [(illegible] impossible the . . . . (Common partnership dissolved Hamacto) [illegible] Conflict not as nations but as empires sympathy for Belgium France—Nations yet despite their vicious imitation of the ————— Quote N. *Amer*, 330)"
5. Paragraph break inserted at beginning of sentence.
6. Paragraph break inserted at beginning of sentence.
7. Paragraph break inserted at beginning of sentence.
8. Word deleted following "is": "the".
9. "still" replaces original "yet".
10. Words deleted following "month": "the editor will pardon my italics."
11. "Europe at Armageddon," *North American Review* 1142 (September 1914):321-22.
12. Ibid., 330-31.

Index

Jackson, Walter A., xlv
James, William, xxxiii, xxxvii
Japanese, social assimilation of, 94
Johnson, Guy, xlv
Johnson, Mordecai, xlii
Jordan, Winthrop, 1

Kallen, Horace Meyer, xxxvi, xxxvii
Kennedy, Sinclair, 31
Kinship, 20–22, 34
Kousser, J. Morgan, xlix
Kraal, 51
Ku Klux Klan, xxi

LaPouge, Georges, 93–94
Law, contribution to restricted status, 48, 52
Lenin, V.I., xxvii
Levinson, Daniel, xlii
Literature, racial consciousness and, xxxii, xxxvi, xlii-xliii, xliv, xlv
Locke, Alain: biography of, xxxv-xlviii; cultural theory of race defined, xliv-xlv
Lodge, Henry Cabot, 29

Mandle, Jay, 1
Marx, Karl, xxvi-xxvii, xxx, xxxii
Marxism, xxxiii, xlvii
Mason, Charlotte, xlvi
McKay, Claude, xlvi
Mead, Margaret, xxiv
Miller, Kelly, xx, xxxiv, xl, xli
Missionarism, 26–28
Moore, Lewis, xx, xl
Moorland, Jesse, xx
Morley, John, 30
Mu-So-Lit Club, xxxiv

National Association for the Advancement of Colored People (NAACP), xx, xxxiv, xl
Nationalism, xliii, 86
Negro Americana, xx
Newman, S.M., xli
New Negro Renaissance, xxxii, xxxiv, xliii, xliv, xlvi

Oxford Cosmopolitan Club, xxxviii

Palmer, George Herbert, xxxvi
Pan Americanism, 31
Park, Robert E., xxxiv, 55
Peonage, 50
Plato, 74
Population, relation to race feelings, 56–57
Populist Revolt, xlix
Powell, Richard, lii
Prejudice: color, 64–65, 68; race, 64, 66–72; social, 54, 57
Primary group, 55

Race: biological theory of, xx, xxi-xxii, xxiv, 5, 12, 13; classification of, 3–4; contacts, 41–58; creeds, xxx, li, 63– 79; fallacies of, 74–76, 78; historical theories of, xx-xxi, 7; inferior vs. superior, 2–3, 4, 22–23; political conceptions of, 20–35; practical conceptions of, 20–35; practices, 41–66; prejudice, 64, 66–72; pride in, xxxii, 57, 97; relations and economics, xlix-1; sense, 20–21; sociological theory of, 11–14; stages of relations, xlix; state of relations in   America, xxi; static vs. changing factors of, 10–11; superiority, 72–73; theoretical conceptions of, 1–14; type, 97–98, 100
Race consciousness, xxi, xxiii, xxxii, 96–98; based on arts and letters, xxi, xxxii, xxxiii, xlv, xlii-xliii; based on cultural ties with African civilization, xxxix, xlv; as a tool of advancement, xxi
Racial conflict, economic competition and, xxvii-xxviii
Racial inequalities: factors determining, 10–11; vs. racial differences, 9
Racial purity, 74, 86
Racism, xxi, xlix; in America, xxx; contemporary views of, l; in democratic societies, xxix; economics

114